OCR SHP GCSE

VIKING EXPANSION c.750–c.1050

CHRISTOPHER CULPIN

SERIES EDITORS:
Jamie Byrom and Michael Riley

DYNAMIC LEARNING

HODDER EDUCATION
AN HACHETTE UK COMPANY

The Schools History Project

Set up in 1972 to bring new life to history for school students, the Schools History Project has been based at Leeds Trinity University since 1978. SHP continues to play an innovatory role in history education based on its six principles:

● Making history meaningful for young people
● Engaging in historical enquiry
● Developing broad and deep knowledge
● Studying the historic environment
● Promoting diversity and inclusion
● Supporting rigorous end enjoyable learning

These principles are embedded in the resources which SHP produces in partnership with Hodder Education to support history at Key Stage 3, GCSE (SHP OCR B) and A level. The Schools History Project contributes to national debate about school history. It strives to challenge, support and inspire teachers through its published resources, conferences and website:
http://www.schoolshistoryproject.org.uk

This resource is endorsed by OCR for use with specification *OCR Level 1/2 GCSE (9–1) in History B (Schools History Project) (J411).* In order to gain OCR endorsement, this resource has undergone an independent quality check. Any references to assessment and/or assessment preparation are the publisher's interpretation of the specification requirements and are not endorsed by OCR. OCR recommends that a range of teaching and learning resources are used in preparing learners for assessment. OCR has not paid for the production of this resource, nor does OCR receive any royalties from its sale. For more information about the endorsement process, please visit the OCR website, www.ocr.org.uk.

The publishers thank OCR for permission to use specimen exam questions on pages 104–105 from OCR's GCSE (9–1) History B (Schools History Project) © OCR 2016. OCR has neither seen nor commented upon any model answers or exam guidance related to these questions.

Note: The wording and sentence structure of some written sources has been adapted and simplified to make them accessible to all pupils while faithfully preserving the sense of the original.

Every effort has been made to trace all copyright holders, but if any have been inadvertently overlooked, the Publishers will be pleased to make the necessary arrangements at the first opportunity.

Although every effort has been made to ensure that website addresses are correct at time of going to press, Hodder Education cannot be held responsible for the content of any website mentioned in this book. It is sometimes possible to find a relocated web page by typing in the address of the home page for a website in the URL window of your browser.

Hachette UK's policy is to use papers that are natural, renewable and recyclable products and made from wood grown in sustainable forests. The logging and manufacturing processes are expected to conform to the environmental regulations of the country of origin.

Orders: please contact Bookpoint Ltd, 130 Park Drive, Abingdon, Oxon OX14 4SE. Telephone: (44) 01235 827720. Fax: (44) 01235 400454. Email education@bookpoint.co.uk Lines are open from 9 a.m. to 5 p.m., Monday to Saturday, with a 24-hour message answering service. You can also order through our website: www.hoddereducation.co.uk

ISBN: 978 1 4718 61109

© Chris Culpin 2017

First published in 2017 by
Hodder Education,
An Hachette UK Company
Carmelite House
50 Victoria Embankment
London EC4Y 0DZ

www.hoddereducation.co.uk

Impression number   10 9 8 7 6 5 4 3 2 1

Year   2021 2020 2019 2018 2017

Cover photo: © Ted Spiegel/Corbis

Typeset by White-Thomson Publishing LTD

Printed in Italy

A catalogue record for this title is available from the British Library.

CONTENTS

INTRODUCTION

Making the most of this book

● Where this book fits into your GCSE history course

The course

The GCSE history course you are following is made up of five different studies. These are shown in the table below. For each type of study you will follow **one** option. We have highlighted the option that this particular book helps you with.

OCR SHP GCSE B

Paper 1 1 ¾ hours	**British thematic study** ● The People's Health ● Crime and Punishment ● Migrants to Britain	**20%**
	British depth study ● The Norman Conquest ● The Elizabethans ● Britain in Peace and War	**20%**
Paper 2 1 hour	**History around us** ● Any site that meets the given criteria.	**20%**
Paper 3 1 ¾ hours	**World period study** ● 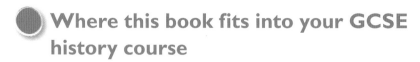 Viking Expansion ● The Mughal Empire ● The Making of America	**20%**
	World depth study ● The First Crusade ● The Aztecs and the Spanish Conquest ● Living under Nazi Rule	**20%**

The world period study

The world period study focuses on a wider world society and the unfolding story of a particularly interesting period in its history. It explores the relationship between different cultures at a time of great upheaval and considers the experiences and perspectives of different individuals and groups in the past.

As the table shows, you will be examined on your knowledge and understanding of the world period study as part of Paper 3. You can find out more about that on pages 100 to 105 at the back of the book.

Here is exactly what the specification requires for this world period study.

Viking Expansion, c.750–1050

The specification divides this world period study into five headings:

Headings	Learners should study the following content:
Homelands	• The Vikings in Scandinavia: landscape, society, and everyday life • Viking ships, seafaring and trade c. 750 • Viking beliefs and rituals
Volga Vikings	• The changing nature of Viking (Rus) trade and settlement in Russia from c. 750 • The nature of Viking trade and interaction with the Arab world • Viking relations with Constantinople and the Byzantine Empire
Raiders and Invaders	• The nature and causes of Viking raids in Britain, Ireland, the Scottish Islands and France, 793–850 • The nature of Viking warfare: warships, warriors and tactics • The 'great heathen army' in England and the establishment of Danelaw', 865–879
Settlers	• The nature and extent of Viking settlement in the British Isles and France • Viking life in Jorvik • The nature and extent of Viking settlement across the Atlantic including Iceland, Greenland and North America
Kings	• Harald Bluetooth, Jelling and the conversion of the Vikings to Christianity • Svein Forkbeard and his invasions of England • Cnut's Anglo-Scandinavian Empire, 1016–1035

You need to understand:

● The expansion of the Viking world from c. 750 to c. 1050, with a particular focus on warfare, trade and settlement.

You need to be able to:

● Identify, describe and explain events and developments relating to the nature of the Vikings' expansion and their interactions with different cultures.

The next two pages show how this book works.

How this book works

The rest of this book (from pages 8 to 99) is carefully arranged to match what the specification requires. It does this through the following features::

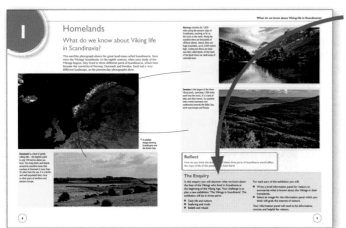

Enquiries

The book is largely taken up with five 'enquiries'. Each enquiry sets you a challenge in the form of an overarching question.

The first two pages of the enquiry set up the challenge and give you a clear sense of what you will need to do to work out your answer to the main question. You will find the instructions set out in The Enquiry box, on a blue background, as in this example.

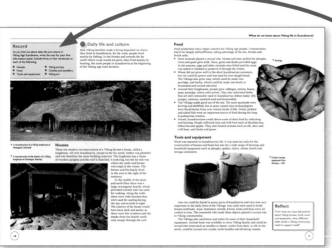

Record tasks

From that point, the enquiry is divided into three sections. These match the bullet points shown in the specification on page 3. You can tell when you are starting a new section as it will start with a large coloured heading like the one shown here. Throughout each section there are 'Record' tasks, where you will be asked to record ideas and information that will help you make up your mind about the overarching enquiry question later on. You can see an example of these 'Record' instructions here. They will always be in blue text with blue lines above and below them.

Reflect tasks

At regular intervals we will set a 'Reflect' task to prompt you to think carefully about what you are reading. They will look like the example shown here. These Reflect tasks help you to check that what you are reading is making sense and to see how it connects with what you have already learned. You do not need to write down the ideas that you think of when you 'reflect', but the ideas you get may help you when you reach the next Record instruction.

Review tasks

Each enquiry ends by asking you to review what you have been learning and use it to answer the overarching question in some way. Sometimes you simply answer that one question. Sometimes you will need to do two or three tasks that each tackle some aspect of the main question. The important point is that you should be able to use the ideas and evidence you have been building up through the enquiry to support your answer.

Closer looks

Between the enquiries you will find pages that provide a 'closer look' at some aspect of the theme or period you are studying. These will often give you a chance to find out more about the issue you have just been studying in the previous enquiry, although they may sometimes look ahead to the next enquiry.

We may not include any tasks within these 'closer looks' but, as you read them, keep thinking of what they add to your knowledge and understanding. We think they add some intriguing insights.

One very important final point

We have chosen enquiry questions that should help you get to the really important issues at the heart of each section you study, but you need to remember that the examiners will almost certainly ask you different questions when you take your GCSE. Don't simply rely on the notes you made to answer the enquiry question we gave you. We give you advice on how to tackle the examination and the different sorts of question you will face on pages 100 to 105.

Who were the Vikings?

This painting by the illustrator Peter Jackson appeared in the children's magazine *Treasure* in 1970. It shows fierce Viking raiders storming ashore on the coast of Britain.

Reflect

How has Peter Jackson made the Vikings seem particularly fierce?

▲ 'Vikings', by the illustrator Peter Jackson, from the children's magazine *Treasure*, 9 May 1970

The image of the Vikings as fierce warriors is based on historical reality, although there is no evidence that they wore helmets with wings or horns! The word 'Viking' means raider and certainly some Vikings did plenty of raiding, as you will discover in this book. But the Vikings were much more than warriors and raiders.

When our study begins, around AD750, the Vikings had a rich and varied culture in their homelands of Scandinavia. They worked as farmers, fishermen, traders, weavers, woodworkers, stone-carvers and metalworkers. Some Vikings built fine houses and adorned themselves with beautiful jewellery. They worshipped a range of pagan gods and created wonderful stories about life and the universe.

In the period 750–1050, the Vikings became highly-skilled shipbuilders, constructing vessels which could carry them huge distances across wild and dangerous seas. Some Vikings from what would later become Norway and Denmark sailed west. They built new lives for themselves in lands across the North Sea and the Atlantic Ocean. Vikings from Sweden established long-distance routes in the east and settled along the vast rivers of what would later become Russia.

The examples opposite give an impression of what Vikings might have been doing across the Viking world in June 983.

Reflect

What do the examples reveal about the extent of Viking expansion and the diversity of Viking life?

Across the Viking world, June AD983...

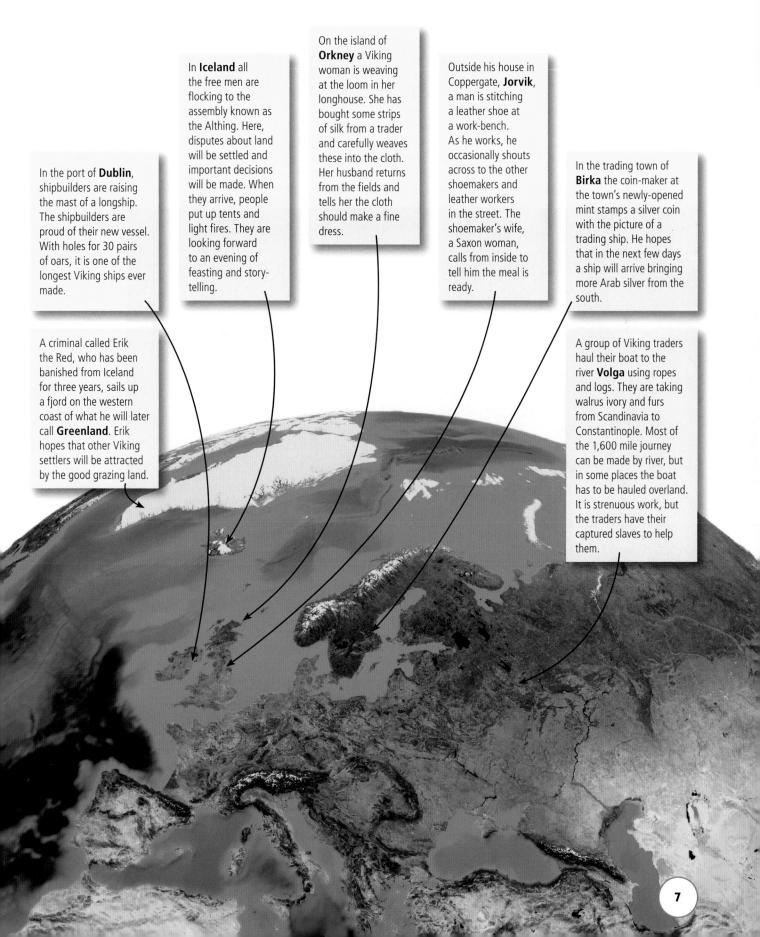

In the port of **Dublin**, shipbuilders are raising the mast of a longship. The shipbuilders are proud of their new vessel. With holes for 30 pairs of oars, it is one of the longest Viking ships ever made.

In **Iceland** all the free men are flocking to the assembly known as the Althing. Here, disputes about land will be settled and important decisions will be made. When they arrive, people put up tents and light fires. They are looking forward to an evening of feasting and story-telling.

On the island of **Orkney** a Viking woman is weaving at the loom in her longhouse. She has bought some strips of silk from a trader and carefully weaves these into the cloth. Her husband returns from the fields and tells her the cloth should make a fine dress.

Outside his house in Coppergate, **Jorvik**, a man is stitching a leather shoe at a work-bench. As he works, he occasionally shouts across to the other shoemakers and leather workers in the street. The shoemaker's wife, a Saxon woman, calls from inside to tell him the meal is ready.

In the trading town of **Birka** the coin-maker at the town's newly-opened mint stamps a silver coin with the picture of a trading ship. He hopes that in the next few days a ship will arrive bringing more Arab silver from the south.

A criminal called Erik the Red, who has been banished from Iceland for three years, sails up a fjord on the western coast of what he will later call **Greenland**. Erik hopes that other Viking settlers will be attracted by the good grazing land.

A group of Viking traders haul their boat to the river **Volga** using ropes and logs. They are taking walrus ivory and furs from Scandinavia to Constantinople. Most of the 1,600 mile journey can be made by river, but in some places the boat has to be hauled overland. It is strenuous work, but the traders have their captured slaves to help them.

7

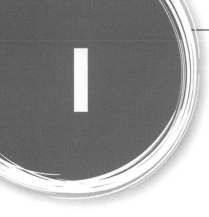

Homelands

What do we know about Viking life in Scandinavia?

This satellite photograph shows the great land mass called Scandinavia. Here were the Vikings' homelands. In the eighth century, when your study of the Vikings begins, they lived in three different parts of Scandinavia, which later became the countries of Norway, Denmark and Sweden. Each had a very different landscape, as the present-day photographs show.

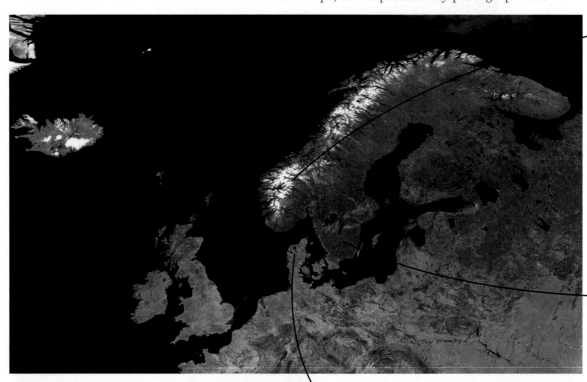

◀ A satellite image showing Scandinavia and the British Isles

Denmark is a land of gently rolling hills – the highest point is only 170 metres above sea level. The many inlets and islands around its coastline mean that nowhere in Denmark is more than 35 miles from the sea. It is a fertile and well-populated land, close to other parts of northern and western Europe.

Norway stretches for 1,600 miles along the western edge of Scandinavia, reaching as far as the Arctic in the north. Along the coastline there are thousands of offshore islands. Inland, there are huge mountains, up to 2,400 metres high. Cutting into these are deep sea inlets called fjords. At the head of the fjords there are small areas of cultivable land.

Sweden is the largest of the three Viking lands, stretching 1,000 miles north into the Arctic. It is a land of lakes and thick forests. Its coastline looks mainly eastwards and southwards towards the Baltic Sea, north east Europe and Russia.

Reflect

How do you think the landscape of these three parts of Scandinavia would affect the ways of life of the people who lived there?

The Enquiry

In this enquiry you will discover what we know about the lives of the Vikings who lived in Scandinavia at the beginning of the Viking Age. Your challenge is to plan a new exhibition 'The Vikings in Scandinavia'. The exhibition will be in three parts:

● Daily life and culture
● Seafaring and trade
● Beliefs and rituals

For each part of the exhibition you will:

● Write a brief information panel for visitors to summarise what is known about the Vikings in their homelands.
● Select an image for the information panel which you think will grab the interest of visitors.

Your information panel will need to be informative, concise and helpful for visitors.

Record

As you find out about daily life and culture in Viking Age Scandinavia, write the text for your first information panel. Include three or four sentences on each of the following:

- Houses
- Food
- Tools and equipment
- Viking society
- Clothes and jewellery
- Viking art

Daily life and culture

How Viking families made a living depended on where they lived in Scandinavia. By the coast, people lived mainly by fishing. In the forests and towards the far north where crops would not grow, they lived mainly by hunting. But most people in Scandinavia at the beginning of the Viking Age were farmers.

▲ A reconstruction of a Viking longhouse at Moesgard, Denmark

▼ A reconstruction of the interior of a Viking longhouse at Stavangar, Norway

Houses

These are modern reconstructions of a Viking farmer's house, called a longhouse. All over Scandinavia, except in the far north, timber was plentiful and was therefore the main building material. The longhouse has a frame of wooden uprights and the roof is thatched. It looks big, but the far end was where the cattle and horses were kept in the winter. The farmer and his family lived in the area to the right of the entrance.

In the middle of the stone and earth floor there was a large rectangular hearth, which provided warmth and was used for cooking. Along the walls there were wide benches that were used for seating during the day and as beds at night. The interior of the house would have been dark and smoky as there were few windows and the smoke from the hearth could only escape through the roof.

Food

Food production was a major concern for Viking Age people. Communities had to be largely self-sufficient, taking advantage of the sea, forests and fertile soils.

- Farm animals played a crucial role. Horses and oxen pulled the ploughs. Cows and goats gave milk. Hens, geese and ducks provided eggs. In the autumn, pigs and other animals were killed and the meat was salted or smoked to preserve it through the winter.
- Wheat did not grow well in the short Scandinavian summers, but rye could be grown and was used for sour-dough bread. The Vikings also grew oats, which could be made into porridge, and barley, which could be made into broth or fermented and turned into beer.
- Around their longhouses, people grew cabbages, onions, beans, peas, parsnips, celery and carrots. They also cultivated herbs that are still commonly used in Scandinavian dishes today: dill, juniper, caraway, mustard seed and horseradish.
- The Vikings made good use of the sea. The main sea-foods were herring and shellfish, but at some coastal sites archaeologists have found bones from over twenty kinds of fish. Dried, pickled and salted fish were an important source of food during the long Scandinavian winters.
- Inland, Scandinavians could obtain some of their food by collecting and hunting. People collected nuts and wild fruit such as blackberries, bilberries and apples. They also hunted animals such as elk, deer and wild boar, and ducks and geese.

▼ Herrings

Tools and equipment

Wood was essential in Scandinavian life. It was used not only for the construction of houses and boats but also for a wide range of farming and household equipment such as ploughs, spades, chairs, chests, bowls and storage containers.

◄ Kitchen storage equipment from Norway, c. 830

Iron ore could be found in many parts of Scandinavia and iron was very important in the daily lives of the Vikings. Iron nails were used to build houses and boats. Axes, hammers, swords, knives, locks and keys were all crafted in iron. The ironsmith who made these objects played a crucial role in Viking communities.

The Vikings also used bone and antler for some of their household equipment. Animal bone was available to every Viking family and could be turned into items such as needles or skates. Antler from deer, or elk in the north, could be turned into combs, knife handles and drinking vessels.

Reflect

From what you have discovered about Viking homes, food, tools and equipment, what different skills would a Viking community need to support itself?

Viking society

The people of Viking Age Scandinavia can be divided into three broad social groups according to their place in society.

- **Thralls** were slaves. They were captured in war, or forced into slavery by getting into debt, or by being the child of a slave. Thralls did all the heavy work on the farm and could be bought and sold. They could sometimes buy their freedom, or be freed by their master.

- **Bondi** were freemen who usually owned their own land. Bondi had a say in all local matters, decided at a meeting called a *thing*. They varied in wealth, but a typical bondi would have three or four thralls to help him. He would be expected to turn out to fight when called upon, to have his own weapons, and know how to use them.

- **Jarls** were important landowners and warriors. A jarl was the 'chief' of the bondi in his area. In return for the bondis' loyalty and readiness to fight for him, the jarl looked after their needs. He led his warriors in the *viking* (sea-borne raids) and was expected to reward them. It was from the jarls that the first kings would emerge during the Viking Age.

Viking women

The roles of men and women were separate, and Viking society was male-dominated. A woman could not be a bondi or a jarl, nor take part in the *things,* nor appear in court. A girl was expected to obey her father and then to obey her husband when she married – usually aged about twelve. However, women still played a crucial role in Viking life and some historians think that they were better placed than women in other societies at this time.

A woman ran the household, making sure that the food lasted during the long, cold, dark winter. She milked the cows and goats, made butter and cheese, dried and smoked meat and fish for storage. She cared for her children and the elderly. She was expected to know about herbs for making medicine. She made all the clothes, spending long hours spinning, weaving, dyeing and sewing the cloth – it is estimated that making one linen tunic, from cutting the flax to the finished garment, took 400 hours of work.

The key hanging from her belt symbolised a woman's power over the home. Viking men were away a lot, on hunting or fishing expeditions, trading or raiding abroad for months, even years at a time. During this time, the woman was in charge of the farm as well as the household, overseeing the work of the thralls, looking after the animals and seeing that the crops flourished and were safely harvested.

▶ Viking keys displayed in a museum

Reflect

How does the key worn by a Viking woman symbolise her role in Viking society?

Clothes and jewellery

It is hard to be certain about Viking clothes because fabrics do not survive very long in the ground, but fragments discovered by archaeologists have enabled them to make some good guesses about what the Vikings looked like. Finds of Viking jewellery can also help us to imagine their appearance.

Men

It seems that men usually wore a long-sleeved undershirt made from linen or wool. This was pulled on over the head and reached to just above the knees. We think the men wore loose trousers, with a tunic reaching below the waist, and a cloak over the top, fastened at the shoulder with a big brooch, like the one opposite. Most men wore a belt, to carry a purse or a knife. There were different styles of shoes, but most seem to have been ankle boots or slip-ons, fastened with ties or toggles.

Women

Women wore an under-dress, reaching to their ankles, with a pinafore-style dress on top, fastened on each shoulder with an oval brooch. These brooches are distinctively Viking and have been found wherever Viking women lived. They sometimes had a necklace of beads hanging between them, like the one here. Women wore a belt round their waist, with a leather pouch for things such as sewing needles and fire-steels – pieces of iron used to produce sparks to start the fire. Their shoes were similar to those worn by men.

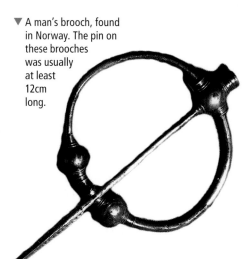

▼ A man's brooch, found in Norway. The pin on these brooches was usually at least 12cm long.

Reflect

What does the size of the man's brooch suggest about the cloaks worn by Viking men?

◀ A woman's oval brooches and necklace

Vikings took care over their appearance. Women and men wore their hair long and men often had beards and moustaches. Both men and women carried wood, bone or antler combs, often beautifully decorated. The clothing of wealthier Vikings was decorated with patterned edges woven in bright colours. Archaeologists have even found gold and silver thread in some fragments of material. Jarls and wealthier bondi sometimes wore rings, arm-rings and neck-rings made from silver and gold.

Viking art

The Vikings were skilled carvers in wood, metal and stone. Much of the finest art was found on the possessions of wealthy jarls who used it to show their status and power. The most common design was based on strange animals mixed with interlacing shapes. You can see three remarkable examples of Viking art here.

Carving from the Oseberg ship

Many Viking artists worked in wood as it was cheap and relatively easy to carve. However, very little wooden carving has survived. This beautiful example from the early ninth century shows a detail of the carving on the Oseberg ship (see Closer look 1, page 24). The interwoven animals twist and turn, gripping the edge of the ship and each other.

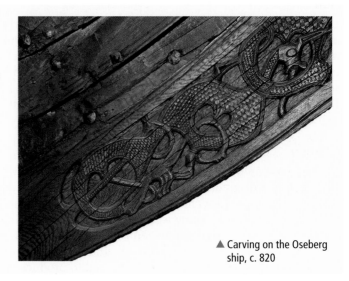

▲ Carving on the Oseberg ship, c. 820

Reflect

Do you think the same person would have fixed the ship's main timbers and carved these patterns?

The Mammen axe head

This magnificent iron axe head, inlaid with silver, was placed in a grave at Mammen in Denmark at the end of the tenth century. The axe head was richly decorated on both sides and was probably used in ceremonial parades. The design on this side of the axe shows interlaced plant tendrils or the roots of a tree. On the other side is a similar design, with a bird's head in the centre.

◀ The decorated Mammen axe head

The Broa horse bridle mount

This decorated bronze mount was fixed to the leather bridle of a horse. It dates from around AD800 and was found with similar pieces in the burial mound of a wealthy Viking jarl. At the top you can see a strange face and what seem to be two birds. Some people think that this could be the god Odin (see page 21). Six stylised animals are designed in the ovals on the bridle mount. Like the carving on the Oseberg ship, the animals grip the edges and are enmeshed in the interlocking pattern.

▶ Horse bridle mount from Broa

Runestones and runes

Runestones are found all over Scandinavia. By far the greatest number – 2,500 – are in Sweden. There are 250 in Norway and about 100 in Denmark. Runestones were set up, usually in a public place, as memorials to friends or relatives. The earliest runestones in Scandinavia date from the fifth century, but most were carved between 950 and 1100. When they were first made, runestones were often brightly coloured, but now only the carving remains.

The letters, often following a snaking course over the stone, are runes. This is the 16-letter runic alphabet, called the 'futhark', from the first six letters.

Runes were designed to carve short messages on wood or stone and are read from right to left. They were used all over Germany and northern Europe from the second century until the arrival of Christianity brought the Latin alphabet to Scandinavia in the late tenth century. The runic inscriptions are the only writing we have from the Vikings themselves, so are very useful to historians.

This is one of two Swedish runestones that were placed in a marshy isolated area in the early eleventh century. The runic inscription is carved on two long serpents around the edge of the runestone. It reads:

> Danr and Húskarl and Sveinn and Holmfríðr, the mother and (her) sons, had this stone erected in memory of Halfdan, the father of Danr and his brothers; and Holmfríðr in memory of her husbandman

Near the top of the runestone is a Christian cross and beneath it are several stylised animals. The animal heads are usually in profile with slender, almond-shaped eyes and long necks that are interwoven into a pattern.

▲ The runic alphabet

▼ The Lingsberg runestone

Reflect

What similarities can you see in the examples of Viking art on these pages?

Record

When you have written the text for your information panel on daily life and culture, select an image to include on the panel. You could use one of the images on pages 10–15 or find an alternative image online. Explain why you have selected the image.

Seafaring and trade

The pictures on pages 8–9 show how important water was to the people of Scandinavia. Denmark includes many islands and the mainland is deeply cut into by sea inlets. The many offshore islands on Norway's coast provide a route north avoiding large stretches of open sea – the 'north way'. Sweden has a long coastline with many islands, but also a large number of inland lakes. Water transport was an essential part of living in Viking Age Scandinavia.

Ships

It is not surprising that in the early centuries AD the people of Scandinavia had developed skills in seafaring and boat building. By the eighth century they were building specialist vessels for different purposes: fishing boats, trading ships for coastal travel, warships and ships for longer sea journeys. Of course, very few Viking Age ships have survived, but we can learn a lot from some remarkable discoveries.

▲ A replica of the Kvalsund ship in the Bergen Maritime Museum, Norway

The Kvalsund ship

In 1920 an amazing discovery was made in a bog in Norway – the Kvalsund ship. The archaeologists who investigated the ship dated it to around AD690. The Kvalsund ship was about 18 metres long and 3 metres wide. It was rowed by twenty oarsmen, ten on each side. Like many Viking ships it had a shallow draught, enabling it to travel quite a long way up rivers or muddy estuaries. Such a ship did not need a harbour or a jetty to land, but could be pulled onto a beach or bank, and pushed back into the water when it was time to leave.

The archaeologists who studied the Kvalsund ship made two important discoveries:

- It had a steering oar (rudder) attached to one side of the stern. This allowed the ship to change direction and could be easily pulled up in shallow water.

- The shape of the Kvalsund ship suggests that it almost certainly had another crucial development – a sail. Sails had been used by Mediterranean seafarers for centuries, but there is no evidence of Scandinavian ships using them before the seventh century. It seems that Scandinavians stuck with rowing vessels, which could be easily manoeuvred along the coasts. No direct evidence of a sail had been found on the Kvalsund ship but this picture of a sailing vessel from a runestone proved that the Scandinavians were using sails by the eighth century. In the following centuries, it was this innovation, more than any other, that led to expansion of Viking culture beyond Scandinavia.

▶ An eighth-century picture on a runestone from Tjangvide, Gotland, Sweden

The Skuldelev ships

From around AD980, the town of Roskilde, near Copenhagen, was an important trading port. Its only access to the open sea is a long, narrow channel. Sometime in the eleventh century, when Roskilde was facing an attack from the sea, several ships were deliberately sunk at the mouth of this channel, in order to block it.

Following local fishermen's stories, divers in the 1950s located these wrecks at a place called Skuldelev and in 1962 a proper archaeological investigation began. What they found was extraordinary: five Viking Age ships from the eleventh century, in a remarkable state of preservation, emerged from the mud.

What was left of the ships after 1000 years under water was carefully studied in order to find out about the different types of Viking Age ships and the skills of shipbuilders.

Replicas of all of them have been built using only the tools and materials available in the Viking period.

▼ A replica of the *skeid* found at Skuldelev. It was made in 2008

The five Skuldelev ships were:

- a wide and sturdy cargo-vessel known as a *knarr* – with its crew of between six and eight, the ship could carry goods on long-distance trading voyages
- a small cargo ship, suitable only for coastal trade
- a small fishing boat from western Norway
- a small warship known as a *snekkja* which was 17 metres long and could carry up to 30 Vikings
- a large warship known as a *skeid*. This fast sea-going ship was 30 metres long and could carry up to 80 Vikings. Such a ship could reach the coast of Britain in a couple of days.

It is unlikely that large warships like the one found at Skuldelev would have been used by the Vikings in 750. However, archaeologists think that by the late tenth century shipbuilders were producing a range of vessels, including larger ocean-going ships. The few Viking Age ships that have survived reveal the wide range of ships that were used by the Vikings. They also demonstrate the skill of Scandinavian shipbuilders. It was the development of the sailing ship in Scandinavia and the skills of seamen that opened up possibilities for trading, raiding and settlement across the oceans.

Reflect

1 What do you think the people who made the replica of this Skuldelev ship only used tools and materials available in the Viking age?
2 What clues in the image show that this replica is a *skeid*?

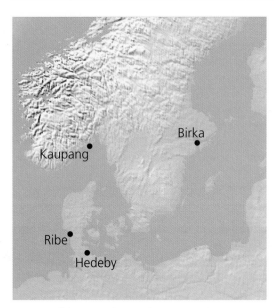

▲ A map of the main Viking trading towns in the eighth century

Trading towns

By AD750 Scandinavian sailors had visited, and were familiar with, eastern England, Scotland and the Orkney islands, the coast and islands of Frisia (the Netherlands), north Germany and the south coast of the Baltic Sea. Some took part in violent raids, but mostly they went to trade.

Better ships and increasing trade in the eighth and ninth centuries led to the setting up of the first trading towns in Scandinavia. The trading towns were established in places that were easy to reach by sea and land. They contained a safe harbour, a market place, workshops and houses. Often they were under the protection of a king or powerful jarl. In the eighth century, three important trading towns were Hedeby, Birka and Kaupang.

Hedeby

The first Scandinavian trading town was at Ribe, in Denmark (see map), where a market was established by 710. However, in 808 Godfred, one of the earliest kings of Denmark, transferred the merchants to his new market site at Hedeby. The new town was on a fjord with easy direct access to the Baltic Sea, but close to rivers flowing into the North Sea and the main land route running through the centre of Denmark.

Modern aerial photographs still show Hedeby clearly. A semicircular earth and timber wall, 5 metres high, surrounded the town, with entrances through gates to the north and south, and from the harbour on the fjord. Wood-paved streets were laid out on a regular perpendicular grid. As well as visiting merchants, workers in several crafts had workshops in the town, making cloth, pottery and jewellery. Early trade was often by barter, but soon coins were being minted at Hedeby to make business transactions easier. This artist's illustration shows what Hedeby might have looked like at its peak in about 876. With a population of perhaps 1,500 people, it was the largest community in Scandinavia at the time.

▼ An aerial photograph of the present-day site of Hedeby in Denmark

▼ An artist's reconstruction of Hedeby in the ninth century

Birka

In Sweden, a similar trading site was established at Birka in the second half of the eighth century. Birka is on an island in Lake Mäleren, part of a string of lakes that lead eastwards to the Baltic Sea and westwards further into Sweden. The area was close to the lands of the kings of central Sweden and the market was under their patronage.

There was a small fort, with houses and workshops leading down to the lake. In the ninth century the population of Birka was about 700. The importance of shipping to the growth of the town is shown by the ship on this coin, which was minted at Birka.

▶ A silver coin from Birka

▲ An aerial photograph of the site of Birka in Sweden

Kaupang

The first market town in Norway was at Kaupang, where merchants gathered to trade from ships drawn up along the sides of a narrow fjord. Trading there began in the 780s and lasted until the early tenth century, although some archaeologists have doubted whether it was always occupied all the year round.

Excavation has revealed rows of small houses and workshops, and the population has been estimated at about 600. Kaupang was also known as *Skíringssalr* – 'the shining hall', perhaps named after its lord's residence on the hill behind the town.

Archaeological finds give clues as to what businesses were carried on at Kaupang. Jewellery seems to have been important, with moulds for casting lead jewellery, pieces of amber and nearly a thousand glass beads. Archaeologists have also found slag and cinders from iron-working, and loom weights from weavers.

Record

Write the text for your information panel about Viking seafaring and trade. This should include a short paragraph on ships and another on trading towns.

Select an image to include on the information panel. You could use one of the images on pages 16–19 or find an alternative image online. Explain why you have selected the image.

▼ An artist's reconstruction of Kaupang in the ninth century

Beliefs and rituals

By the eighth century the rest of Europe had been Christian for several centuries, but not the Vikings. The Vikings' pagan beliefs made their culture very different from that of their Christian neighbours.

There are no detailed descriptions of Viking Age religious beliefs and rituals in Scandinavia. Everything written about Viking pagan religion comes from Christian sources. The Icelandic *eddas* (folk stories) tell us something of Viking beliefs, but these were composed in the thirteenth century by Christian descendants of Vikings. Archaeologists can tell us about sites that might have a religious significance, but we can only guess at what went on there. Despite these limitations, Christian sources and archaeology allow us to piece together some features of Viking paganism.

Stories about the universe

Viking pagan beliefs were very different from those of organised religions. There was no 'holy book', no prophet, no priests, no moral code telling people how to behave. But spirituality – a belief in forces beyond human powers – was fundamental to Viking life, and can be heard in the stories that the Vikings told about the universe.

The *eddas* tell us that Vikings believed that the centre of the universe was a giant sacred ash tree, *Yggdrasil*, which spanned the cosmos. The gods lived on one level, called *Asgard*, while the world of humans was called *Midgard*. In the sea around this world lived the *Midgard* serpent. In an underworld, called *Hel*, lived giants, trolls, elves and other horrible creatures, who sometimes visited the human world, perhaps in the form of an eagle, a squirrel or a cockerel. Three females, called the *norns*, lived at the roots of *Yggdrasil* and controlled the past, present and future.

Vikings believed that the world would end with the final battle of *Ragnarok*. A fire would sweep across the whole world, destroying the gods and all humans. Some historians have suggested that this gave the Vikings a fatalistic attitude to life: humankind was doomed anyway, so you might as well live adventurously and die fighting. That way, your good name, the respect and honour you earned, ensured that you lived on after your death through the stories told about you.

◀ A stone carving from Gotland, Sweden, showing Odin riding on *Sleipnir*

Viking gods

The Vikings did not worship a single all-powerful deity, but honoured a large number of gods and goddesses. The gods all had various characteristics and weaknesses, like humans but more so. The three most important gods were Odin, Thor and Frey.

▼ A lucky charm in the shape of Thor's hammer

Odin was the supreme god. He was the god of war and the dead, but also of poetry and wisdom. He had one eye, having traded his other one in order to drink from the well of knowledge. Powerful, but unpredictable, he was often accompanied by his ravens, *Huginn* and *Munnin*, who flew all over *Midgard* and told him about what was happening in the world. Odin rode an eight-legged horse, called *Sleipnir*. All Vikings who died bravely in battle were collected by his female helpers, the *Valkyries*, and taken to feast for ever in Odin's hall, *Valhalla*.

Thor was a very popular god, and many Vikings wore his emblem, a hammer called *Mjöllnir*, crafted by the dwarfs. Over a thousand of these have been found, from all over the Viking world. Thor was the god of thunder and lightning, and rode over the clouds in a chariot drawn by goats. He was also the god of crops and plague. Thor was straightforward and reliable and so was also the god of law and order.

Frey was the third main Viking god. He was the god of favourable weather needed to ensure a good harvest. For this reason he was associated with wealth and general prosperity. Frey was also chief of the fertility gods. Freya was Frey's twin sister. She was the goddess of love and fertility, but also of sorcery, spells and magic.

These Viking gods have given us three of our days of the week: Odin (Wednesday), Thor (Thursday) and Frey (Friday).

Private rituals

The Viking gods were not worshipped, but people made offerings to them. Offerings were also made to local and family gods and to the spirits of places with sacred power, such as groves of trees, waterfalls, rocks or wells. Some offerings took place at home or at a simple altar of piled stones known as a *hörgr*. The gods were called on at the three great moments in family life: birth, marriage and death.

- **Births** were dangerous in Viking times; women called on Freya to help them and gave thanks to her when their baby was safely delivered. After nine days the baby was sat on the father's knee and he gave it a name, so admitting her or him to the family. Names might include references to favourite gods.
- **Marriage** was partly a business arrangement between the two fathers of the couple, which took place at betrothal. But the marriage itself involved calling on the gods to bless the couple, followed by feasting and drinking which was expected to last at least three days.
- **Death.** The dead were mostly buried near to settlements and their graves were visited frequently. Contact with the ancestors was important to the well-being of the family. If ancestors were treated with the proper rituals, they were thought to give their blessings to the living, ensuring happiness and prosperity. If the rituals were not followed, the dead were thought to haunt the living and bring bad fortune.

Reflect

Why is it hard to be sure about Viking beliefs and rituals?

Religious sites

Written sources and archaeology suggest that the Vikings sometimes had religious gatherings in special places, led by a jarl, or king. At Uppsala, in Sweden, a great festival was held which all inhabitants of the Swedish provinces were required to attend. This gathering had several functions, apart from the religious rituals. A market was held, and important court cases were heard. Christian visitors reported the existence of a 'temple', and archaeologists have found the remains of a large building, 100 metres long, with burial mounds nearby.

There is a similar site in Denmark, at Lake Tissø, (the lake of Tyr, a god of war). Many weapons have been found in the lake as offerings to Tyr. Some of the swords found had been deliberately bent, so that they could never be used again. By the lake, there are the post-holes marking out a very large hall, in which the remains of feasting have been found. Next to a marketplace nearby, there are wells, in which the skulls and limb bones of horses, bulls, cows, pigs, dogs and goats had been placed.

▲ A ritually bent Viking sword

▶ Post-holes of the large hall at Lake Tissø

Archaeologists interpret these sites, and others elsewhere in Scandinavia, as gathering places for major rituals. Offerings were made to the gods by the sacrifice (known as *blot*) of lots of animals, such as pigs, dogs and bulls, but particularly horses. Twigs were dipped in the horses' blood in order to spatter it over the altars. Some archaeologists have suggested that human sacrifice may also have been practised by the Vikings.

Offerings were followed by a huge feast, provided by the jarl as an opportunity to show off his wealth and power. These feasts were the only time Vikings ate horsemeat. Many toasts were drunk to the gods. The large buildings described by the Christian visitors and found by archaeologists were likely to have been the halls where the feasts were held.

Burials

Most of the evidence for Viking religious rituals comes from the graves and cemeteries that have been discovered throughout Scandinavia. The Vikings disposed of the dead in a range of ways. Some corpses were cremated – ashes could be placed in a container, heaped in a pile or scattered across a site. Other Vikings were buried – skeletons are found in a range of positions, with or without coffins, sometimes alone and at other times in family groups or in a large cemetery.

Many Viking graves contained grave goods. These often reflected the wealth and status of the dead person. In one grave at Birka in Sweden the deceased was surrounded by all kinds of goods: sword, knife, spearheads, axe, arrow-heads, shield bosses, mounts, stirrups, knife, whetstone, 28 counters, 3 dice, 3 weights, ring-pin, silver mount, buckle, comb, bits. At his feet were the dismembered remains of two horses.

The presence of grave goods in many burials suggests that the Vikings believed in an afterlife where the objects would be needed. Some Vikings were buried in ship-shaped graves like the ones below at Lindholm in Denmark, while others were buried in actual ships to carry them to the afterlife.

▼ The Lindholm ship graves. The graves range in date from c. 500 to c. 1050

Record

Write the text for your information panel about Viking beliefs and rituals.

Select an image to include on the information panel. You could use one of the images on pages 20–23 or find an alternative image online. Explain why you have selected the image.

Review

Select five artefacts or sites which you think should be included in the exhibition. These should help to give visitors a broad understanding of the Vikings in Scandinavia. Write a short paragraph for each artefact or site explaining why you have chosen it.

The Oseberg ship burial

▲ The excavation of the Oseberg ship burial, 1904

In the autumn of 1903 a farmer at Oseberg in eastern Norway discovered a large burial mound on his land. The following summer a team of archaeologists from Sweden and Norway began to excavate the site. They were amazed to uncover a remarkably well-preserved Viking ship containing the remains of two women and a huge range of grave goods. The soil in the burial mound was very damp and this meant that the ship and its contents had survived nearly intact. The Oseberg ship burial is one of the most important finds from the Viking Age.

The ship

Archaeologists dated the Oseberg ship burial to 834. The ship itself was a very fine vessel. Built of oak around the year 820, it was nearly 22 metres long and over 5 metres wide. With 15 oar-holes on each side, there were spaces for 30 rowers, and the mast shows that the ship could also be sailed. Archaeologists found some of the oars, a gang-plank and a bailing bucket on the ship. The Oseberg ship reveals the extraordinary skills of Viking boat-builders and woodcarvers. The stern and bow of the ship are beautifully carved with animal shapes (see page 14) and the bow ends in a spiralling serpent's head.

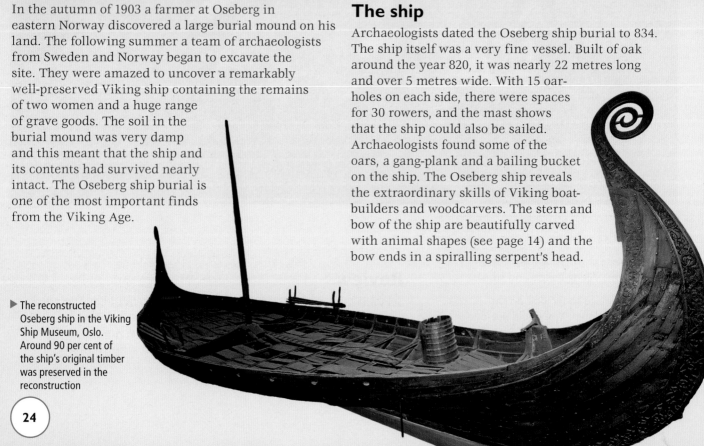

▶ The reconstructed Oseberg ship in the Viking Ship Museum, Oslo. Around 90 per cent of the ship's original timber was preserved in the reconstruction

The burials

At the centre of the Oseberg ship, in a tent-shaped wooden burial chamber behind the mast, archaeologists discovered the skeletons of two women. The bodies had been placed on a bed made up with bed linen, and the wall of the chamber had been decorated with beautiful woven tapestries. Research on the skeletons revealed that the older woman was between 70 and 80 when she died while the younger woman was just over 50. The older woman wore a red woollen dress with a lozenge pattern and a fine linen veil. On top she wore a tunic, which included strips of silk. The younger woman wore a plainer blue wool dress. Clearly, this was a high-status burial, but we do not know who the women were, or how they died. Was one a queen or a princess? If so, which one? Was the other a loyal slave, sacrificed with her mistress?

The grave goods

Any gold and silver which had originally been in the Osberg ship burial had been taken by grave-robbers centuries before, but what made the discovery so remarkable was the huge range of grave goods which had been preserved in the damp earth of the burial mound. These included:

- the skeletons of animals including 14 horses, an ox and three dogs
- personal items such as clothes, shoes, combs and jewellery
- kitchen utensils including three decorated buckets, three iron pots, basins and spoons
- household goods such as oil lamps, chests and five weaving looms
- farm tools including a fork for moving animal dung
- plums, apples, blueberries and a small leather pouch containing cannabis
- five beautifully carved animal heads – these may have been from an item of furniture or a symbol carried in a procession
- three splendid ornate sleighs, originally painted in bright colours
- a beautifully carved oak cart. The back was decorated with carvings of cats and on the front the carvings showed a man being attacked by serpents.

Whoever planned the Oseberg ship burial had gone to a lot of trouble and expense to ensure that the two women had everything they might have needed in the afterlife.

▲ One of the five carved animal heads

◀ A bucket with brass decoration

▶ The oak cart

2

Eastward expansion

How should we describe the Volga Vikings?

This is the River Volga, the longest and widest river in Europe. It begins north of what is now Moscow and flows south to the Caspian Sea (see map on page 29). In the eighth century, Vikings from Sweden began to explore the River Volga, making their way south to meet the great trade routes of central Asia. Some Vikings even crossed the Caspian Sea and travelled still further on the overland route to Baghdad. Other Viking traders travelled down the River Dnieper to reach the Black Sea and eventually the great Byzantine city of Constantinople. Historians have labelled the Scandinavians who explored and traded in the east 'the Volga Vikings'.

The driving force for these long and difficult journeys was trade, but the Volga Vikings were more than adventurers and traders. In the ninth and tenth centuries, they settled and ruled a huge territory along the great river networks of the east. The history of the Volga Vikings in the east is less well-known than the story of the Vikings in the west, but it is an important and fascinating part of Viking expansion in the period 750–1050.

The Enquiry

In this enquiry you will find out about:

- Viking trade and settlement in the east
- The Volga Vikings and the Arab world
- The Volga Vikings and the Byzantine Empire

Your challenge is to become an expert historian on the Volga Vikings. You will prepare for a radio interview that will feature in a new documentary programme: *The Volga Vikings*. The producer of the programme will send you some questions about the three different aspects of Viking expansion in the east. Your task is to write the notes that you can use to answer the producer's questions.

Record

Here are the questions that the producer has sent you for the first part of the programme, on Viking trade and settlement in the east:

1 When and how did the Vikings begin their eastward expansion?
2 What challenges did they face in the east?

3 What were the main goods that they traded?
4 What do we know about Viking settlers and rulers in the east?

As you find out about the expansion of the Vikings along the river systems of the east, make notes to help you answer each of these questions.

Beginnings

It was mostly Vikings from Sweden who travelled east. As you can see on the map opposite, Sweden's coasts face east and south to the Baltic Sea. A short voyage across the Baltic brought them into the Gulf of Finland. From there, at some point in the eighth century, Swedish traders began to explore the rivers in what is now Russia. They sailed up the River Neva to Lake Ladoga, then to Staraya Ladoga on the River Volkhov. This was the beginning of Viking expansion in the east.

Staraya Ladoga

From the late eighth century, Staraya Ladoga was an important trading town for the Vikings. Archaeologists have found evidence of Viking metalwork, jewellery and boat building in the settlement. Hundreds of Viking burial mounds like the ones in the photograph below dot the landscape around Staraya Ladoga, suggesting that the town had permanent Scandinavian residents there over a long period of time.

Founded in about 750 by the local Slav population, Staraya Ladoga was a meeting point of many different traders including the Vikings. The talk there was of the exotic goods in the rich bazaars of Baghdad and Constantinople far away. These prospects, and especially the lure of silver, led the Vikings to venture on from Staraya Ladoga.

▼ Viking burial mounds at Staraya Ladoga

Heading south

The journey south from Staraya Ladoga was long, difficult and dangerous. The Viking traders travelled along the River Volkhov to Lake Ilmen. From there, they could sail down other rivers, but they were forced to haul their boats overland to the River Dnieper. In one stretch, the Dnieper had 40 miles of rapids, only passable in late summer when the water was lower. The Vikings faced similar challenges on the rivers further east. Between the Volkhov and the Volga Rivers, ships had to be emptied of their trading goods and everything was dragged over land. Throughout the journey, but especially during these long hauls overland, there was the danger of robbers. Viking traders had to be armed and watchful, guarding their valuable goods and themselves.

The distances involved were enormous. From Staraya Ladoga to the Black Sea is 1,200 miles by river. It was then a further 400 miles across the Black Sea to Constantinople – a total of over 1,600 miles. Recently, some Swedes took 89 days to travel from Sweden to the Black Sea in a reconstructed Viking ship. They showed that the Vikings could not have set out, taken time to trade and returned home in one season, so must have stayed away for at least two years. The journey down the Volga, across the Caspian Sea and overland to Baghdad was even further. The Viking traders who reached Baghdad were 2,500 miles from their homeland in Sweden.

Reflect

Find the two different routes that the Vikings took from their homelands in Sweden to:

- Constantinople, capital of the Byzantine Empire
- Baghdad, capital of the Abbasid Caliphate.

What challenges did they face on these journeys?

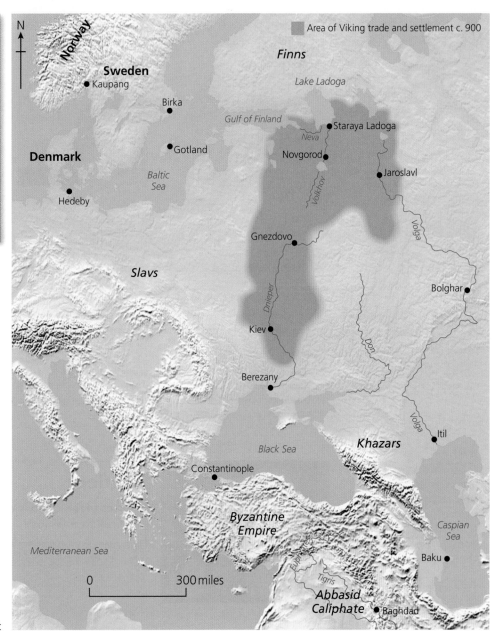

▶ The Vikings in the east

Viking trade

Scandinavia lacked gold and silver, but it had some desirable goods that were not found elsewhere. The products that the Viking traders took south had to be high in value, small in bulk and able to withstand long journeys.

Swords

▲ A Viking sword

The Vikings were skilled metalworkers and made very good swords. They also obtained high-quality swords from the Franks to trade in the east. Arab and Byzantine traders paid high prices for these swords.

Honey

The Arabs and Byzantines greatly valued honey as a sweetener for different foods and drinks. Scandinavia produced plentiful supplies of good honey. This was an ideal product as it took up little room and could be sold for high prices.

▲ Honey

Furs

Scandinavia was rich in animals whose skins and furs were very attractive to the citizens of Constantinople, where the winters could be quite cold. Seal skin and furs such as fox, sable, ermine, polar bear and beaver could all fetch high prices. A coat made from the white fur of arctic foxes would have been particularly prized.

▲ Arctic fox

Walrus ivory

▼ Walrus

Walrus live off the northern coasts of Norway and their tusks provided a source of fine ivory which could be carved into beads, rings and jewellery. Walrus ivory could fetch high prices in the markets of Baghdad and Constantinople.

Falcons

Many Arabs were fanatical falconers. They had their own hawks, but a trained peregrine falcon from Scandinavia, the fastest bird in the sky, could command a high price.

◀ Falcon

Slaves

This slave-collar was discovered by an archaeologist at the Viking market at Birka. The Vikings were well-known for trading in slaves. Some were brought from Scandinavia. Others were collected as the Viking traders travelled south. The Volga Vikings might raid a village as they passed, taking goods or slaves, as 'tribute' for not burning down the houses of the Slavs.

▲ Slave-collar

Amber

Amber was the fossilised resin of certain trees which grew around the Baltic. Once hardened it could be carved and polished, like these pendants, glowing orange to catch the eye of a buyer.

▶ Amber pendants

Reflect

Which of these goods would have been the most difficult to transport?

Viking settlers and rulers

As early as the eighth century, the Vikings began to establish a series of small settlements along the river systems of western Russia. These were places where they could stop to repair the boats, collect supplies of food and pick up news of the river trade. At first they were rough-and-ready places where the Vikings met and traded with the local Slav population and other traders.

The people in the east named the Vikings 'the Rus', a version of the Finnish name for Swedes. Gradually, the Rus population increased and the settlements became small towns. By the middle of the ninth century, the Vikings were so well established along the river routes that they were able to control the towns and surround them with strong defences.

Some 400 archaeological sites across the region have revealed the Viking presence through finds of Scandinavian brooches, neck-rings, beads, swords and boat burials. The Scandinavians in these Slav lands were a tiny minority, an élite of merchants and rulers who took 'tribute' from the Slav population. Gradually, it seems that these Vikings became more like their Slav subjects whom they ruled. They married Slav women, gave their children Slavic names and adopted Slavic ways of living.

▼ Viking beads found in Russia

Novgorod and Kiev

The Rus towns of Novgorod and Kiev became particularly important to the Vikings because they allowed them to control the river routes from north to south.

By 860 the Vikings had built a major fortified centre at Novgorod ('New Fortress'), ruled by a Viking called Riurik. Around 882, Riurik's heir, Oleg, became ruler of Kiev. He joined together the existing villages on the banks of the Dnieper to create an important trading town. Some historians think that Kiev eventually became the foundation of the state of Russia which Oleg's heirs ruled for over 700 years.

Vladimir, the Rus ruler of Kiev from 978 to 1015, brought about a crucial change in 988. He became a Christian and cemented his alliance with Byzantium by marrying the Emperor's sister. The Orthodox Christian Church took hold in Rus territory, and with it came the Greek alphabet and Byzantine law, political style, education, music and literature. The language of the Church, however, was neither Greek nor Scandinavian, but Slav.

Vladmir's son, known as Yaroslav the Wise, ruled the Rus state of Kiev from 1019 to 1045, increasing its power and wealth. He built the Golden Gate of Kiev, completed in 1024, with a Byzantine-style church behind. The gate was dismantled in the Middle Ages, but it was rebuilt by the Russians in 1982.

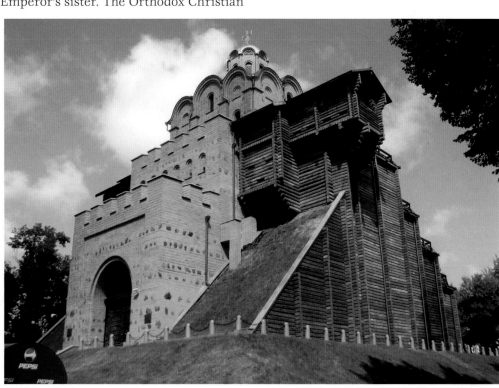

▶ The Golden Gate of Kiev

Record

Here are the questions that the producer has sent you for the second part of the programme, on the Volga Vikings and the Arab world:

1 What was the relationship between the Volga Vikings and the Arab world?
2 Which particular products attracted the Vikings to Baghdad?
3 How did the Muslims see the Volga Vikings?

As you find out about the expansion of the Volga Vikings into the Arab world, make notes to help you answer each of these questions.

Baghdad and the Arab world

In the ninth century the Volga Vikings established a strong trade link with the Arab world. The boldest and most adventurous traders travelled all the way down the Volga, across the Caspian Sea and then overland to Baghdad by camel. In the 840s one Arab writer described the Rus merchants as

> … a sort of European, bringing beaver skins and black fox fur and swords from the furthest part of their land … They reach the Caspian Sea and sail out, putting in wherever they want. Often they bring their wares by camel … to Baghdad, where Slavonic eunuchs interpret for them.

It is not difficult to see why the Volga Vikings were attracted to Baghdad. The city had been founded by the Abbasid caliph al-Mansur in AD762. As you can see below, al-Mansur decided on a striking design for his capital city: Baghdad was a circular city. At its centre was the great mosque as well as the caliph's palace, military buildings, and beautiful gardens. Four roads led from the centre, through the main gates of the city and out through the suburbs.

▼ The city of Baghdad in the tenth century

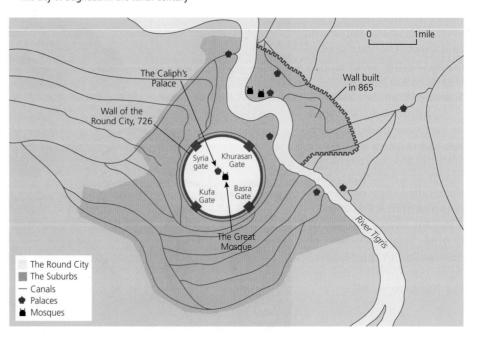

By the tenth century, Baghdad had a population of over a million people. In the districts beyond the round city, craftsmen and merchants built workshops, bazaars, houses, mosques and hospitals. Baghdad was an important world centre of knowledge and learning. The Abbasids built libraries and gathered texts from different cultures. Baghdad's scholars translated these texts and made advances in science, mathematics, astronomy and medicine.

The Volga Vikings who travelled to Bagdad must have marvelled at the sights of the city, but most of all they were interested in the different goods in its many bazaars. Baghdad had strong connections with the wider Muslim world, which stretched from central Asia to southern Spain. It was also connected to the long-distance trading routes to Asia and China. The Volga Vikings were eager to trade with Baghdad's merchants as they knew that luxury goods from the wider world could fetch high prices in Scandinavia.

▼ The Abbasid Empire, c. 850

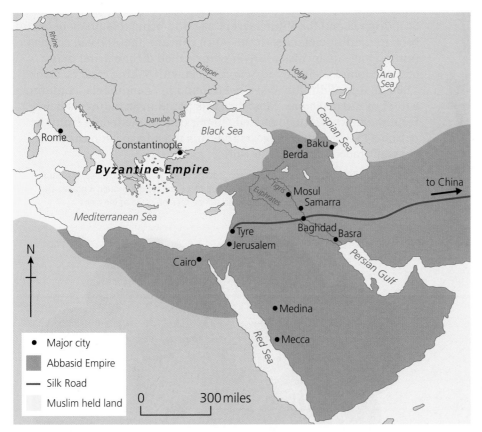

The Viking relationship with the Arabs was not always peaceful. In 912 a Viking fleet crossed the Caspian Sea and raided Baku. In another raid in 943, the Vikings captured and held the Abbasid city of Berda for several months. Nearly 30 runestones in Sweden were made in memory of Vikings who were killed in a raid in Serkland (the land of the Saracens, as the Arabs were called) led by Ingvar the Far-Travelled in 1041. The runes on this stone read:

> Tola had this stone raised in memory of her son Haraldr, Ingvarr's brother. They travelled far for gold, and in the east gave food for the eagle [were killed] in Serkland.

▶ A runestone from Gripsolm, Sweden

▼ Fragments of silk from the Oseberg ship burial

Silk

Scandinavians loved the spices and other unusual goods from far away that they found in the bazaars of the Muslim traders. In particular, they wanted the luxurious fabric silk, which had been transported thousands of miles along the Silk Road from China. Imagine how a Viking, used to rough woollen clothes and heavy furs, would have felt on touching this light, soft, smooth cloth. Silk does not survive the passage of time well, but these fragments were found sewn as a fringe to the cloak of one of the women on the Oseberg ship (see page 24). What is left of the colours and the patterns give just a hint of how gorgeous they must have looked when newly unpacked by a Viking merchant, straight back from his travels.

Silver

Most of all, the Vikings wanted silver. There were no silver mines in Scandinavia and the Vikings were eager to bring this precious metal back to their homelands. In the tenth century, the Abbasid caliphs minted huge quantities of silver coins called dirhams and many of these found their way to Scandinavia with Viking traders. Over 1,000 hoards of dirhams have been found in Scandinavia, containing a total of 228,000 coins. Most dirhams found in Scandinavia date from the tenth century. Indeed, 30 per cent of them date from the period 940–60, which suggests that this must have been the peak years of trade with the Arab world.

▼ Part of a hoard of 470 dirhams found near Stockholm. As you can see, these were large, handsome coins. Each dirham is as big as a 50p piece and weighs around 3 grams. The Arabic writing and images of the caliph can still be seen on some of the coins

▼ This silver ring, with an Arabic dedication to Allah, was recently found at Birka, in Sweden, in a woman's grave dating from about 850

The Scandinavians did not begin to mint their own coins until the tenth century so Arab dirhams were widely used as currency by Viking merchants. However, much Arab silver, including dirhams, was almost certainly melted down and turned into wearable items. Rich Vikings wore their wealth as arm-rings or neck-rings, usually of a fixed weight of 100 or 200 grams.

The Arab texts

We can learn a lot about the Volga Vikings from archaeological discoveries, but it is fortunate that more than twenty Arabic texts from the period 830–1050 contain descriptions of the Volga Vikings. One text, in particular, provides some interesting insights into the Volga Vikings, as seen from an Arab perspective. It was written in 921 by an Arab lawyer called Ibn Fadhlan who travelled along the Volga as part of an Abbasid embassy. Ibn Fadhlan recorded his impressions of the Rus. He certainly included some shocking details in his descriptions.

The sexual behaviour of the Volga Vikings, described by Ibn Fadhlan

They have no modesty when it comes to defecating or urinating and do not wash themselves when intercourse puts them in a state of ritual impurity. They do not even wash their hands after eating. Indeed, they are like roaming asses.

They come from their country in the North, anchor their ships in the Volga River, and build large wooden houses on its banks. In every such house there live ten or twenty, more or less. Each man has a couch, where he sits with the beautiful girls he has for sale. Here he is as likely as not to enjoy one of them while a friend looks on. At times several of them will be thus engaged, each in full view of the others. Now and then a merchant will come to a house to purchase a girl, and find her master thus embracing her, and not giving over until he has full had his will.

The burial practices of the Volga Vikings, described by Ibn Fadhlan

I was told that when their chiefs die, they consume them with fire. When I heard that one of their leaders had died, I wanted to see this myself. First they laid him in his grave, over which a roof was erected, for the space of ten days, until they had completed cutting and sewing his funeral clothes.

His family asks his girls and servants, 'Which one of you will die with him?' One will answer: 'I'. When the day had come that the dead man and the girl were to be committed to the flames, I went to the river where his ship lay, but found it had already been drawn ashore. The dead man lay at a distance in his grave, from which they had not yet removed him. Next they brought a couch, placed it in the ship, and covered it with Greek cloth of gold, wadded and quilted, with pillows of the same material. … A woman, whom they call the 'Angel of Death', came and spread articles on the couch. It was she who was to slay the girl. They drew the dead man out of the grave and clothed him. They carried him into the ship, seated him on the quilted covering, supported him with the pillows, and brought strong drinks, fruits, and herbs to place beside him. Finally they brought a cock and hen, slew them, and threw them in, too. It was now Friday afternoon, and they led the girl to an object they had constructed which looked like a door-frame. They lifted her and lowered her several times. Then they handed her a hen, whose head they had cut off. They gave her strong drink and admonished her to drink it quickly.

After this, the girl seemed dazed. At this moment the men began to beat upon their shields, in order to drown out the noise of her cries, which might deter other girls from seeking death with their masters in the future. They laid her down and seized her hands and feet. The old woman known as the Angel of Death knotted a rope around her neck and handed the ends to two men to pull. Then with a broad dagger she stabbed her between the ribs while the men strangled her. Thus she died. The family of the dead man drew near, and taking a piece of wood, lit the ship. The ship was soon aflame, as was the couch, the man, the girl, and everything in it.

Reflect

Archaeological discoveries of Viking burials in the east confirm Ibn Fadhlan's account of animal and human sacrifice. What beliefs do you think lay behind these practices?

The Volga Vikings and the Byzantine Empire

To Vikings in the east, the city of Constantinople was known simply as *Miklagard* – the Great City. The Roman Emperor Constantine had moved the capital of the empire here in AD330. It was still recognisably a Roman city, as the illustration of Constantinople in about the eighth century below shows. Constantinople was protected by twelve miles of high walls and huge towers. A long aqueduct supplied the city's half a million inhabitants with clean water. Constantinople was a Christian city with many fine churches and other buildings. But what most attracted the Viking traders were the city's bazaars, which were packed with exotic goods.

The Golden Horn, safe harbour

The Forum of Constantine

The chariot-racing arena, the Hippodrome

Record

Here are the questions that the producer has sent you for the third part of the programme on the Volga Vikings and the Byzantine Empire:

1 What attracted the Vikings to Constantinople?
2 What was the relationship between the Vikings and the Byzantines?

As you find out about the expansion of the Volga Vikings and the Byzantine Empire, make notes to help you answer each of these questions.

Reflect

Which aspects of Constantinople do you think would have most impressed the Vikings?

▼ A reconstruction of Constantinople in the eighth century

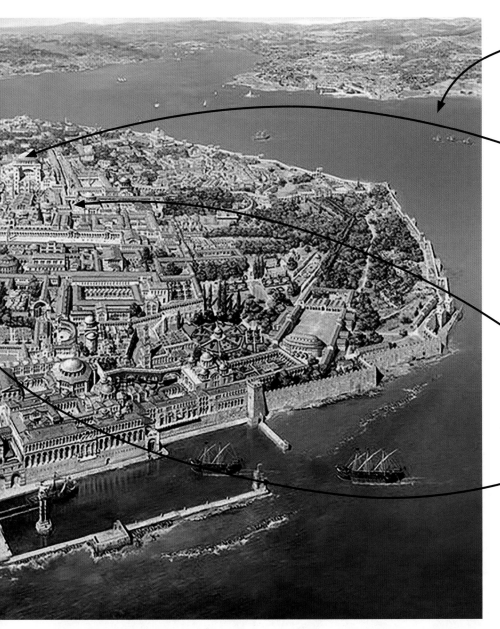

The Bosphorus, leading north to the Black Sea and south to the Mediterranean Sea

The great church of Holy Wisdom, Hagia Sophia. Its huge dome dominated the skyline of Constantinople. Inside, thousands of candles and lamps illuminated the beatiful gold and blue mosaics.

Baths. An aqueduct brought clean water into the city. This was stored in underground cisterns and was used for public as well as private baths.

The Emperor's Palace. This was the main residence of the Emperor and the centre of imperial administration. From the great hall shown here, the palace buildings extended over six terraces leading down to the shoreline.

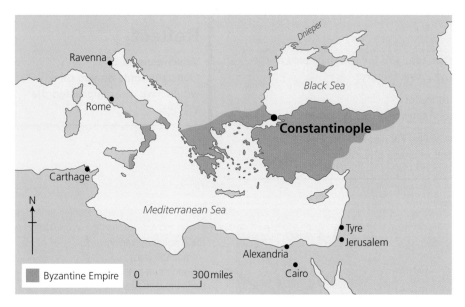

In the ninth century the Byzantines controlled much of the eastern Mediterranean, from what is now southern Italy, to Greece and Turkey. Merchants brought goods from north Africa and the Middle East to Constantinople's bazaars. The Viking merchants must have found the trading opportunities astonishing. Products which were unknown in Scandinavia, such as wine, olive oil, silk, embroidered cloth, fruit, spices and semi-precious stones, such as carnelian and quartz, were all available in Constantinople.

▲ The Byzantine Empire, c. 1000

Traders and raiders

The first Vikings visited Constantinople in 839. Rus envoys visited Emperor Theophilus and seem to have established friendly relations. Then, in 860, the Vikings attacked Constantinople with a fleet said to be 200 ships strong. Even with a large force, there was little chance of the Vikings defeating the Great City but violence enabled them to negotiate a favourable trade agreement with the Byzantine emperor. The Vikings continued to raid and trade in the Byzantine Empire through the tenth century.

In 907, Oleg, the founder of Kiev, launched another attack on Constantinople, from the sea. He was driven off, and was happy to negotiate a trade treaty in 911. This laid out careful rules for the behaviour of Viking Rus merchants in Constantinople. It also included the provision for free baths for the Viking merchants as well as places to repair their ships.

Oleg's treaty lasted for 30 years, until his son Igor began to attack Constantinople again in the 940s. The Vikings were defeated by the Byzantine secret weapon called 'Greek fire', a form of napalm. Many Vikings were burned to death in their ships. Those who jumped into the sea to escape the flames often drowned in their heavy armour.

▼ 'Greek fire' in action, from a twelfth-century manuscript

Igor negotiated another trade treaty in 945. This stated that the Rus could only enter Constantinople in groups of fewer than 50 and without any weapons. It allocated free accommodation for the Rus in the suburbs of Constantinople and limited the quantities of silk they could buy each year. It also arranged that the Rus would fight for the Byzantines. The treaty was sealed with a gift from Igor to the Emperor of furs, wax and slaves. In the 950s the Vikings dominated trade in the city.

The Varangian Guard

From the mid-ninth century, some Scandinavian warriors known as Varangians joined the armies of the Byzantine emperor. In the late-tenth century the emperor formed a new élite bodyguard. It was known as the Varangian Guard because it incuded a large number of Vikings. In the picture below you can see members of the Varangian Guard defending the emperor in Constantinople. We can tell that they are Vikings because of their axes and their three-pointed flags.

▼ Members of the Varangian Guard defending the emperor in Constantinople. An illustration from the Skylitzes Chronicle, late eleventh century

Review

The producer has sent you a final question that she would like you to answer in the radio interview for the documentary on the Volga Vikings:

● Overall, how do you think we should sum up the Volga Vikings?

Write two or three bullet point notes to help you answer this question.

Work with a partner. One of you should be the producer of the new radio documentary on the Volga Vikings and the other should be the expert historian. Perform the interview for the documentary.

The Spillings Hoard

The Swedish Island of Gotland in the Baltic Sea played an important role in the eastern trade of the Vikings. In the ninth century, the most important Viking harbour on Gotland was at Bogeviken in the north. Close to Bogeviken, a runestone commemorates a Viking trader who drowned in the rapids of the Dnieper River south of Kiev. The many hoards of silver found in the area provide further evidence of Viking trade in the east.

It was not unusual to find a Viking silver hoard on Gotland, but in July 1999 two archaeologists searching for coins at Spillings Farm near Bogeviken were amazed by the strength of signal on their metal detector. They had discovered the world's largest hoard of Viking silver – the Spillings Hoard. The discovery attracted much media interest and the Spillings Hoard now has pride of place at the Gotland Museum.

The Spillings Hoard consisted of three separate chests, two containing silver and a third containing bronze. These had been buried under the floor of a workshop some time after 870. The largest chest contained 40 kg of silver: 312 bangles, 20 bars, 30 arm-rings, 20 finger-rings and over 10,000 coins. The silver was obviously valued for its weight because the arm-rings had been bundled into standard Viking weights. Many of the coins had slashes in them, probably made to test the purity of the silver.

Of the total 14,295 coins found at Spillings, 14,200 were Arab dirhams. The Spillings Hoard is remarkable evidence of the vast wealth that the Viking trade in the east brought to Scandinavia in the eighth century.

▼ The location of the Spillings Hoard as found in 1999

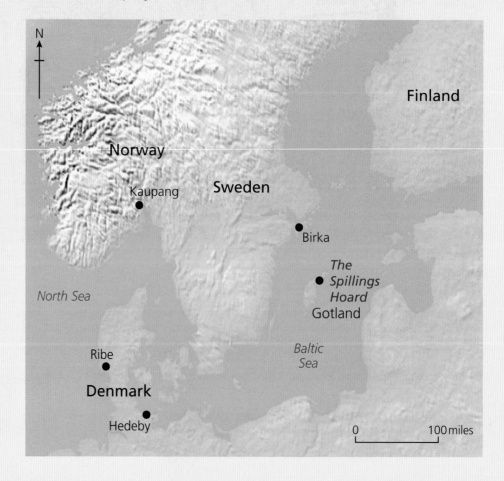

◀ A collection of
weighed bangles.
Part of the Spillings
Hoard

3

Raiders and invaders

How did the Vikings attack western Europe?

▼ Lindisfarne

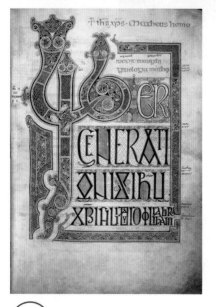

◀ A page from the Lindisfarne Gospels

This is Lindisfarne, off the coast of Northumberland. There was an important monastery here from the seventh century, founded by Aidan, a Celtic saint. By the eighth century, Lindisfarne had become one of the holiest places in Britain. The monastery was particularly special because its monks included scholars and talented artists. This is a page from the Lindisfarne Gospels, beautifully written and illustrated at the monastery around the year 710.

On 8 June 793, ships from Norway suddenly arrived at Lindisfarne and Viking warriors attacked the monastery. They ransacked Lindisfarne, stealing the monastery's treasures of gold, silver and silk. Monks who tried to stop the Vikings were killed or taken as slaves. Somehow, the Lindisfarne Gospels survived and can still be seen in the British Library.

The Viking raid on Lindisfarne in 793 was deeply shocking to the people of Christian Europe. The Anglo-Saxon Chronicle gives some idea of how terrible it was. The monastic scribe who recorded the event saw it as a judgement from God:

> Terrible portents came about in the land of the Northumbrians, and miserably afflicted the people; there were immense flashes of lightning and fiery dragons were seen flying in the air, and there immediately followed a great famine, and after that the heathens miserably devastated God's church in Lindisfarne island by looting and slaughter.

For centuries, the Vikings had been developing strong trading links with western Europe, but with the attack on Lindisfarne the traders became raiders. Lindisfarne was just the beginning. In 794 Vikings attacked the nearby monastery at Jarrow. The following year, they raided the holy sites at Iona on the west coast of Scotland and at Rathlin on the Irish coast. In 799 it was the turn of the monastery at Noirmoutier in the Frankish Empire. During the first half of the ninth century, no monastery or trading town along the coasts and rivers of western Europe was safe from Viking raids. Then, in 865, the Vikings became an even greater threat when they launched a full-scale invasion of England.

▼ The 'Warrior Stone'. Part of a gravestone from Lindisfarne, from the end of the ninth century. Some historians think it may depict the raid of 793

The Enquiry

In this enquiry you will find out about three different aspects of the Viking attacks on western Europe in the eighth and ninth centuries:

- Viking raids
- Viking warfare
- The Viking invasion of England in 865

As you know, historical events and situations are usually quite complex, but this does not stop people make simple statements about them. Historians like to challenge simplified history, helping people to understand the complexity of the past. In this enquiry you will add complexity to three over-simple statements about the Viking attacks on western Europe:

- The Vikings attacked western Europe after 793 because they saw monasteries as easy targets. They raided the monasteries and killed many monks.
- The Viking attacks on western Europe succeeded because the Vikings were fierce warriors.
- The Vikings quickly gained control of England when they invaded in 865.

The Vikings attacked western Europe after 793 because they saw monasteries as easy targets. They raided the monasteries and killed many monks.

As you find out about the Viking attacks on western Europe, make a list of bullet points to add complexity to this over-simple statement.

Viking raids

The Vikings have left no written record of their raids on western Europe, but historians have been able to piece together the main phases of the Viking attacks from the chronicles written by Christian monks. It seems that there were four main phases:

- **Phase 1** For more than 30 years after 793 there were many small-scale hit-and-run raids. At first, these raids were carried out by only two or three ships, but the number of ships gradually increased. These raids took place in the summer, avoiding winter storms. The Vikings never penetrated very far inland and their targets were nearly always isolated monasteries on the coast.

- **Phase 2** From around 830, the scale and nature of the Viking raids changed. Larger groups of Vikings began to arrive in western Europe, often in as many as 30 or 40 ships. The number of ships increased steadily over the next twenty years so that by 850, raids could involve as many as 100 ships. These larger forces were more adventurous. They began to travel far inland down navigable rivers and to attack trading towns as well as monasteries.

- **Phase 3** From around 850, the Vikings began to set up winter camps in places that they could easily defend. In the 850s, they over-wintered at Thanet in the Thames estuary and in the winter of 852–53 they formed a camp on the River Seine near Rouen. 'Over-wintering' meant that the Vikings could begin their raids in the early spring as they did not have to wait for the winter storms to end.

- **Phase 4** In 865 the scale of the attacks changed completely. In that year a large Viking army invaded England. The Viking raiders had become invaders (see pages 56–59).

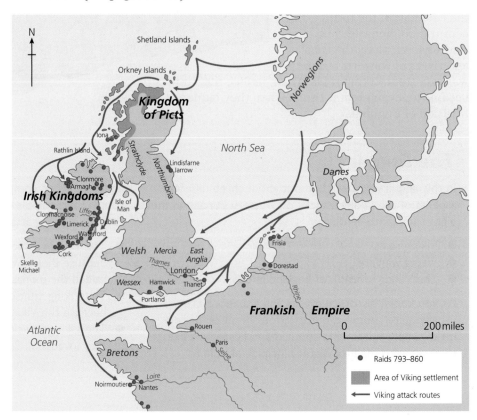

▲ A map of the early Viking raids in western Europe

The causes of the Viking raids

No one is entirely certain why the Viking attacks on western Europe began so suddenly. Several possible explanations were offered at the time. Dudo of Normandy, for example, writing in about 1020, said that the Vikings had too much sex, producing too many children, so some had to leave home and settle elsewhere. In about 1070, Bishop Adam of Bremen suggested that the Vikings were poor, and jealous of the wealth in other lands.

In recent years a range of explanations have been suggested, but there is no real agreement among historians over which is the most convincing. Possible reasons for the Viking attacks include:

Record

Add some bullet points to your list. These should cover the nature and causes of the Viking attacks.

Shortage of good farmland. Although Scandinavia was huge, much of the land could not be cultivated and this meant that there was a shortage of land for farming. Some historians think that there was an increase in population in Scandinavia in the eighth century. More mouths to feed put even more pressure on the scarce amount of good farmland. So, one suggestion for the Vikings' attacks on western Europe is that they travelled overseas to seek out good farmland in more fertile areas and settle there.

The wealth of western Europe. The eighth century was a time of growing trade in western Europe and several market towns had become rich. Scandinavian traders had brought home information about the trading towns and lands of the west. They had seen the isolated monasteries on the coasts and knew that they contained huge quantities of gold, silver and silk. Like the traders, the Viking raiders wanted to obtain western goods, but they decided to steal them instead. They saw the monasteries and trading towns as easy targets.

The growing power of kings in Scandinavia. From the late eighth century, the power of kings in all three Scandinavian lands was growing. Some jarls resented the loss of their independence and power. Honour and personal reputation were important to Viking jarls. One way they could enhance their reputation was by raiding – seizing riches and fighting bravely. Jarls were expected to provide their followers with rewards and opportunities to make their name. The raids gave the jarls a chance to gain glory and to provide their followers with silver and gold.

The weakness of western Europe. In the ninth century, England was divided into a number of small kingdoms: Northumbria, Mercia, East Anglia and Wessex. Scotland and Ireland were made up of areas that were ruled by local chieftains. The opposition to Viking raiders was sometimes fierce and effective, but overall there was no united opposition to the Scandinavian attacks. During the reigns of the powerful king Charlemagne (768–814) and his son Louis the Pious (814–40), the huge Frankish Empire was well defended. However, the divisions and weakness that followed Louis' death made the Frankish Empire vulnerable to Viking attack.

Better ships. Unfortunately, only a few ships from the eighth and ninth centuries have been discovered, but some historians think that advances in ship building enabled the Vikings to attack western Europe. Holes for oars positioned lower down the sides of the ships meant they could travel faster. The use of square sails also gave the ships greater speed. Some historians have argued that these innovations helped to transport Viking raiders across the North Sea to Britain and Ireland.

The attacks on the monasteries

The monasteries of western Europe were easy targets for Viking raiders. The monastic desire to get away from the distractions of ordinary life meant that many monasteries were located at isolated coastal sites. This made them extremely vulnerable to an attack from raiders in ships. Monasteries were not defended sites. Monks did not have weapons so they were unable to resist Viking raiders.

At the time, many Christians thought that the deliberate targeting of monasteries by the pagan Vikings was part of a wider attack on western Christianity. Some historians have argued that the Viking raids were a form of 'psychological warfare'. In other words, they were an attempt to undermine the beliefs of Christians and to show that the Christians' god was vulnerable and not superior to the pagan gods of Scandinavia. However, a more common view is that the monasteries simply offered rich pickings for Viking raiders.

▲ *The Codex Aureus* (the Golden Book), a mid-eighth-century copy of the Gospels from Canterbury

Record

Add to your list with some bullet points about the nature of the attacks on the monasteries.

Rich pickings

Supporters of monasteries liked to make gifts of precious and valuable items. Monastic sites across Europe were full of gold and silver objects, which could be melted down by the Vikings. Larger monasteries imported wine to celebrate Mass and high-quality textiles such as silks for making church vestments. The monasteries often contained plentiful supplies of food. A successful raid on a monastery was like hitting a financial jackpot.

The Vikings soon learned that some things had great value to the Christians, and so they could demand a ransom for them. They probably first noticed religious books because of the gold and silver that was often included on the outer covers, but they later realised that the pages inside also had a value. These illuminated manuscripts were treasured by Christians, who were often prepared to buy them back from the Viking raiders. You can see remarkable evidence of this on a page from the Codex Aureus (the Golden Book) here. The Vikings stole this copy of the four Gospels from Christ Church, Canterbury, probably during a raid in 851. The writing at the top and bottom of the page records how the Anglo-Saxon aristocrat Aelfred and his wife paid the Vikings gold to ensure the book's safe return to Canterbury. The text explains that they paid the Vikings 'because we were not willing that these holy books should remain any longer in heathen hands'.

Viking raiders also realised that it was more profitable to hold monks to ransom, rather than kill them. Many abbots were from aristocratic families who were prepared to pay a high price for their safe return from their pagan captors. In 914 the king paid a ransom of £40 to free the Bishop of Archenfield, captured in a raid on south Wales. Others were not so lucky: when the king refused to pay the huge ransom demand of £3,000 for Aelphege, Archbishop of Canterbury, the poor man was humiliated during a Viking feast by being pelted with ox bones until someone finished him off with an axe.

Viking attacks on Britain

Four years before the attack on Lindisfarne, an incident on the south coast of Britain suggested that the Vikings were becoming a threat. In 789 three ships from Norway landed at Portland off the coast of Dorset. The king's local representative went to meet the Vikings to escort them to Dorchester because he assumed that they were traders. The Vikings turned on him and his party, and murdered them. The attack may have been caused by a misunderstanding, but it made it clear that the Vikings were dangerous.

A year after the raid on Lindisfarne in 793, the Vikings attacked the monastery at Jarrow, further south on the Northumbrian coast (see map on page 44). Jarrow had been established in the seventh century on land given by the Northumbrian king, Ecgfrith. In 794, when the Vikings attacked Jarrow, it was a great centre of learning and was famous across Christian Europe for the beautiful books produced by its monks.

In 795 Viking raiders attacked the monastery on the small Island of Iona off the west coast of Scotland. The monastery had been established by St Columba in the sixth century and the saint's bones were still preserved there when the Vikings attacked. Vikings raiders returned to Iona in 802 and 806 when they killed 68 monks who refused to reveal the whereabouts of St Columba's relics.

Apart from the raids on Iona, there was a lull in Viking attacks on Britain for about 30 years following the first raids in the 790s. Then, in 835, a serious Viking raid on Sheppey in the Thames estuary marked the beginning of nearly 200 years of attacks from Scandinavia, especially Denmark. At first it was mainly southern England that bore the brunt. There were battles in the 830s between the king of Wessex and Vikings in the West Country. By this time the Vikings had discovered that attacking markets yielded greater rewards than monasteries. The prosperous port of Hamwic (Southampton) was raided several times in the 840s. More seriously, the Vikings over-wintered on Thanet, Kent, in 850–51. From there, a large force, said to be 350 ships, attacked London.

Orkney and Shetland

Ships from Norway could reach the Shetland Islands in only two days, with the Orkneys less than another day away (see map on page 44). There were no rich monasteries or trading towns on the islands, but the Vikings were attracted by the good grazing land. In the eighth century, the islands were already occupied by Picts. No records survive of the encounters between the Picts and the Vikings on Orkney and Shetland, but historians think that the Vikings must have taken the islands by force.

We know from archaeological evidence that the Vikings began to settle in Orkney and Shetland around 800. Historians think that the islands may have been the home base for some of the Viking raiders who sailed down the Atlantic coast to raid Iona and the monasteries of Ireland in the early decades of the ninth century.

This hoard was found on St Ninian's Isle, in the Shetlands. There are 28 objects altogether, all of silver: bowls, jewellery and decorated weapons. It was deposited in the late eighth century. Archaeologists think that either Vikings had plundered this silver or that it had been hidden by a local lord to protect his precious belongings from the Vikings.

Reflect

Why was the year 835 a turning point in the Viking attacks on Britain?

▼ A bowl from the St Ninian's Hoard

▲ The beehive huts of the monks at the early Christian monastery of Skellig Michael, off the west coast of Ireland

Viking attacks on Ireland

By the eighth century the Vikings had established trade links with Ireland, but in 795 they sailed to Ireland as raiders. The monastic chronicle, the Annals of Ulster, records that in 795 the Vikings attacked Rathlin Island, off the north coast of Ireland, where the monastery was 'burned by the heathens'.

Over the next 40 years the Vikings attacked many more of Ireland's rich monasteries. First, they attacked religious sites on the south and west coasts, raiding Cork in 822 and the remote monastery on Skellig Michael in 824. Then the raiders turned to monastic sites on Ireland's east coast. In 824 they attacked Bangor, plundered the monastery and killed the bishop.

Around 830, Viking attacks on Ireland began to change. The raiders now came in large fleets and the effects were devastating. Armagh was raided three times in 832 and on Christmas Eve 836 the monastery of Clonmore was burned down. During the 830s the Vikings began to over-winter in Ireland. In 841 they established a *longphort* (a defended settlement) on the River Liffey, which would later become Dublin. The Vikings soon built other *longphorts* on Irish rivers at Cork, Waterford and Wexford, using these as bases for further attacks. By the 840s the Vikings were attacking monasteries far inland. The Annals describe Vikings plundering the land and fighting the local chieftains all over Ireland.

Recent archaeological evidence is beginning to reveal a different story of the first Vikings in Ireland from the one reflected in the Annals. A huge number of Viking skeletons have been discovered under modern Dublin. Some of these pre-date 841 while others are of Scandinavian women. It seems that the *longphort* at Dublin was much more than just a raiding base. The story of the Vikings in Ireland is one of trading as well as raiding. As you discovered in Enquiry 2, raiding and trading were not always distinct activities for the Vikings, particularly when they traded in slaves. The Vikings in Ireland seem to have been different from the settler-farmers in the Scottish islands and the plundering raiders who attacked the English monasteries.

◀ Slave chains used by Vikings.

Record

Add more bullet points to your list to explain how the Viking attacks on the Britain and Ireland were more than simply raids on monasteries.

Viking attacks on the Frankish Empire

In the year 810, a scribe recorded that:

> A fleet of ships from Nordmannia* had attacked Frisia and ravaged all the Frisian islands, defeated the Frisians in three engagements and imposed tribute on them and the Frisians had already paid 100 lbs of silver.
>
> *Nordmannia = Scandinavia

Frisia is now part of the Netherlands but during the rule of Charlemagne from 771 to 814 it was part of the Frankish Empire (see the map on page 44). While Charlemagne lived, the Vikings made few attacks on his lands. Frisia was the place in western Europe with the nearest coast to Denmark. It was the remotest part of the Frankish Empire and therefore the most difficult for Charlemagne to defend. In 810 a Viking attack was driven off, but only after the Frisians had paid much tribute. Charlemagne's death in 814 weakened the Frankish Empire and the Vikings took advantage of this, plundering the important trading town of Dorestad in 834, 835, 836 and 837. However, under Charlemagne's son, Louis the Pious, the Frankish heartlands seemed secure.

When Louis the Pious died in 840 there were bitter struggles between his sons over who should rule, and the Frankish Empire became vulnerable to Viking attacks. In 841 the Vikings took their longships up the River Seine and burnt the town of Rouen. In 843 they sailed up the River Loire and attacked the trading town of Nantes as hundreds of people gathered there for a feast day celebration. The Vikings over-wintered for the first time in 843–44 at Noirmoutier. In 845 there were further raids along the River Seine and the Vikings sacked and looted Paris. The Frankish king, Charles the Bald, bought them off with payment of 7,000 lbs of silver. This was just the first of many payments of 'protection money'. It has been calculated that a total of 44,250 lbs of silver and gold was paid to the Vikings by the Franks in the ninth century.

Charles the Bald, who ruled the Frankish Empire between 840 and 877, took a variety of defensive measures against the Vikings:

- Bridges along the Seine were fortified, to prevent Viking ships from sailing up the river.
- Laws were passed preventing anyone from selling weapons to Vikings.
- Monasteries were encouraged to hide their valuables as soon as they heard of a Viking approach.
- Groups of Vikings were hired to fight off others.

The increasing effectiveness of these measures meant that by the 860s attacks on France became less profitable. This had terrible consequences for England, as you will discover in the final section of this enquiry.

▲ A nineteenth-century portrait of Emperor Charlemagne

Record

Finish your list by including some bullet points to explain how the Viking attacks on the Frankish Empire were more than simply raids on monasteries.

Viking warfare

This image appeared in a magazine called *Look and Learn*, which was popular with children in Britain in the 1970s.

▶ 'The Sea Warriors: Vikings attack a British coastal town', an illustration from *Look and Learn* magazine.

Reflect

How far do you think the illustration presents an accurate image of the Viking raiders?

What questions does the illustration make you want to ask about Viking warfare?

Warriors and weapons

Record

The Viking attacks on western Europe succeeded because the Vikings were fierce warriors.

As you find out about Viking warfare, make a list of bullet points to add complexity to this over-simple statement.

The Vikings were certainly fierce warriors, but we need to discover accurate details of their warfare if we are to produce a complex explanation of how they attacked western Europe after 793. In particular, we need to ignore the stereotypical images found in some magazines, books and websites. Instead, we should turn to the archaeological evidence and written chronicles, asking what these sources can tell us about the weapons, tactics and transport of the Viking raiders.

Figures of warriors carved on grave-markers give us a picture of Viking warriors as they wished to be remembered, and provide some clues about Viking warfare. Several grave-markers in the church at Middleton in North Yorkshire are carved with images of Viking warriors. This crudely carved cross at Middleton shows a Viking warrior in a pointed helmet, surrounded by his weapons.

- On the left you can see a long spear.
- Top right is a shield (much reduced in size).
- Below the shield is a sword.
- Bottom right is an axe.
- Hanging from warrior's belt is a sheath containing a large knife known as a seax.

This array of weapons must have made the Viking warrior a fierce opponent, but there is nothing distinctively Viking about any of these weapons – they were used by fighting men all over Europe.

▲ A Viking warrior carved on a stone cross at Middleton, North Yorkshire

Swords

Over 2,000 Viking swords have been found across the Viking world, mostly in graves. Many of these were elaborately decorated, suggesting the sword was a prized possession. Because swords were expensive items, it may only have been the élite warriors who carried them.

At the beginning of the Viking Age some swords had single-edged blades, but by the ninth century, double-edged swords were used by nearly all Viking warriors. These were single-handed slashing swords, about 90 cm long with a simple cross-guard at the hilt to protect the warrior's hand.

Swords were produced in Scandinavia, but the Vikings particularly valued the high-quality swords made in the Rhineland. These had a strong, but flexible iron blade which would not shatter under an enemy's blows. Three iron rods were twisted and forged together to give more strength to the blade. Then, steel edges were added, sharpened and polished. The centre of the sword was hollowed on both sides, resulting in a strong but light weapon. As you can see in the example on the left, one famous workshop 'signed' their work with the name 'Ulfberht'.

◄ A replica of an Ulfberht Viking sword

Good swords were expensive, passed on from father to son and given special names. Rich Vikings often had their own personal touches added to the hilt, as in this beautiful example found on the Viking trading town of Hedeby in Denmark.

▲ A Viking sword hilt found at Hedeby, ninth century

Axes and spears

Spears and axes were the commonest weapons used by ordinary Vikings. These had a variety of shapes and sizes as you can see in this collection found in the River Thames. At first, Viking battle-axes were simple weapons based on the axes that Scandinavians used for chopping wood. These developed into large, broad-bladed battle-axes, which needed two hands to wield them.

▶ Viking axes and spears from the early eleventh century, found in the River Thames and now on display at the Museum of London. The wooden handles are replicas

A replica of a round Viking shield

Protection

Viking warriors carried a large (1 metre diameter) round, painted shield. This was made of wood, with an iron band round the rim and an iron boss in the middle to protect the grip. Shields have rarely survived in the ground, although examples of the iron boss have been found in many graves.

We know that the Vikings did not wear winged or horned helmets like the ones in the illustration on page 50, so it seems odd that this is such a popular image of Viking warriors. Archaeologists have discovered horns on helmets from Scandinavia in the pre-Viking age. In the nineteenth century, when people in Norway and Sweden began to show great interest in the Vikings, they adopted horned helmets as part of Viking costume. This inaccuracy has continued ever since.

In fact, very few metal helmets from the Viking Age have been found. One (below left) dates from the ninth century and was found in Norway. This is the only reasonably complete helmet to survive from the Viking Age. Archaeologists think that its spectacle eye-pieces may not be typical. The scarcity of archaeological remains of helmets suggests that they were unusual and worn only by the wealthy. Perhaps the ordinary Viking warrior wore a skull protector of hardened leather that has not survived for archaeologists to find.

Carvings from the late Viking Age show that pointed helmets rather than rounded ones were popular by the eleventh century. The warrior's head on the right, protected by a helmet with a nose-shield, was carved from the tip of an elk antler. It is a rare survival. Overall, it seems that most Viking warriors who attacked western Europe wore no helmet at all. We can be sure that no warriors appeared in helmets with wings or horns!

◀ A Viking warrior's helmet found at Gjermundbu in Norway

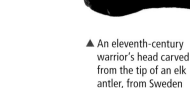

▲ An eleventh-century warrior's head carved from the tip of an elk antler, from Sweden

Tactics

Most Viking raids in the eighth and ninth centuries were carried out by small groups of warriors from the same part of Norway or Denmark. These Vikings were closely bound to each other by ties of loyalty and brotherhood. Kings and chieftains could call on their *Lið* – a fighting unit, sworn to be loyal to each other and to their leader. The warriors expected to work together at whatever needed doing: rowing the longship, fighting, digging fortifications.

When the Vikings attacked defenceless targets such as monasteries they threatened and menaced the monks. The warriors would resort to violence and murder if their demands were not met. Monks who resisted, or who tried to hide the gold and silver objects that the Vikings sought, would be murdered. The sagas describe how they performed the 'blood eagle' ritual on enemies who had particularly annoyed them. This was a ritual dedication to the god Odin, which involved pulling the victim's lungs from his ribcage to create bloody 'wings'.

When the Vikings faced armed opposition, they usually formed a line with their chieftain in the centre, surrounded by a shield wall. The Vikings almost always fought on foot, not on horseback. They sometimes formed a wedge shape to break their enemy's shield wall. The chronicles describe how, going into battle, Vikings shouted war-cries and rattled their shields. Vikings relished fighting and looked for the fame and honour that could be won in fierce hand-to-hand combat. The poem on the right, by the Icelandic Egil Skallagrimsson, was written in about the year 925.

Berserkers

The Icelandic Sagas (see pages 80–81) include descriptions of a group of Viking warriors known as berserkers. The word 'berserker' means someone who wore a bear-skin in battle. These were ferocious warriors who fought crazily, with no care for themselves. One saga described them as 'mad dogs or wolves, they bit into their shields and were as strong as dogs or wolves'. By working themselves up into a frenzy during a battle, the berserkers were said to feel no pain.

There is little evidence for berserkers apart from in the pages of the sagas, and some historians think that they may have been invented by the writers of the sagas to intimidate the enemies of the Vikings. However, archaeological evidence suggests that some warriors made special efforts to look fearsome. For example, these are just two from a full set of deliberately filed teeth that archaeologists found on the skeleton of a Viking warrior in Dorset.

Overall, although the Viking raiders shocked the monastic chroniclers by their failure to respect the holy sites, it is probably the case that the Viking warriors who raided western Europe in the eighth and ninth centuries were no fiercer than Saxon, Pictish, Irish and Frankish warriors of the time.

I've been with sword and spear
Slippery with bright blood
Where kites wheeled. And how well
We violent Vikings clashed!
Red flames ate up men's roofs,
Raging we killed and killed,
And skewered bodies sprawled
Sleepy in town gate-ways

Reflect

How does the poem show the warrior's pride in warfare?

▶ The teeth of a Viking warrior found in Dorset

Warships

It was the Vikings' ships and seamanship that were the most distinctive features of their warfare. Sea transport allowed Viking raiders to reach a wide range of targets along the coasts and up the rivers of western Europe. Their ships also allowed Viking warriors to make a quick getaway with their plunder when the raid was over.

In Enquiry 1 you learned about the early history of ships in Scandinavia, including the crucial developments of sails and the steering oar (see page 16). By the end of the eighth century, the Vikings had developed the ideal vessels for attacking western Europe in lightning raids. These were warships known as longships. The sight of longships off the coasts of Britain, Ireland and the Frankish Empire must have been terrifying to the inhabitants of these lands.

Viking longships had three key features that made them ideal raiding vessels:

- **Speed under sail**. Replica ships built as exact copies of Viking-era longships have reached speeds under sail of 15 knots, even 20 knots in strong winds. These speeds were achievable because the ships were very light and slim, with a length to width ratio of 7:1. Viking raiders could therefore travel long distances and arrive suddenly at their target. While sailing, the crew was resting, in preparation for springing into action.
- **Speed under oars**. At a rowing speed of 5 knots a Viking longship could still get away from any pursuers. Under oars, it could travel into the wind, and go up rivers (the sail could be taken down, the mast lowered and the steering oar lifted in under two minutes). Rowing for long periods was, however, very tiring and a Viking was in no state to start fighting after a long row.
- **Design**. Viking longships did not need a jetty or wharf to land; they could be pulled up on a beach and, being double-ended, pushed out again for a fast getaway. Their lightness meant they had a shallow draught – the depth of water needed before they ran aground. Even a large ship with 60 men on board was able to float in water only a metre deep.

▼ A replica of the Gokstad Viking longship. The original ship was made in the ninth century

Longships were built to carry different numbers of warriors, and were measured by the number of pairs of oars (*rums*), they had. Different sizes of longships were built, of which the smallest was called a *karvi* with less than twenty *rums*. The Oseberg ship (described in the Closer look on pages 24–25) had fifteen *rums* and was not an ocean-going vessel, but built to journey around the coasts, islands and fjords of Scandinavia. A longship of twenty or more *rums* was large enough to handle the open seas. It carried a crew of about 50 and was used in the raids on western Europe.

In the later Viking period, a few very large longships, called *drekke* or dragon-ships, with 30 or more *rums*, were built. The longship on page 17 is called 'Sea Stallion from Glendalough' and is a replica of the largest of the ships found at Skuldelev, off Roskilde in Denmark. You can just see that it had 30 oar holes. This eleventh-century Anglo-Saxon drawing of a Viking *drekke* has just two oars but the ferocious dragon's head is shown very clearly.

Record

Finish your list of bullet points to add more complexity to the over-simplified statement about Viking warfare. Add some points to explain how Viking ships were important to the success of the Viking raids in the eighth and ninth centuries.

▼ A Viking longship, from an eleventh-century manuscript

The Viking invasion of England, 865

In 850 the Vikings had over-wintered on the Isle of Thanet in Kent. This was the beginning of a new phase in the Viking attacks. For over 200 years, the Vikings would never be absent from England. In the fifteen years after 850 the attacks continued. Then, in 865, the Vikings launched a full-scale invasion of England. The Anglo-Saxon Chronicle recorded:

> A great heathen army came into England and took up winter quarters in East Anglia and there they were supplied with horses, and the East Angles made peace with them.

The 'Great Heathen Army'

What the Anglo-Saxons called the 'Great Heathen Army' was led by two Viking brothers, Halfdan and Ivar 'the Boneless'. It is impossible to say with certainty how 'great' the army was: some say as few as 500, others as many as 2,000. It is certain, however, that for the next fourteen years this large force of Danish warriors rampaged across England, over-wintering where they knew they could get supplies and demanding Danegeld (protection money) from the Saxons. By the year 878, the Great Heathen Army had conquered the Anglo-Saxon kingdoms of East Anglia, Northumbria and Mercia. Only Wessex had managed to withstand the Danish onslaught.

▼ The invasion of the Great Heathen Army in 865

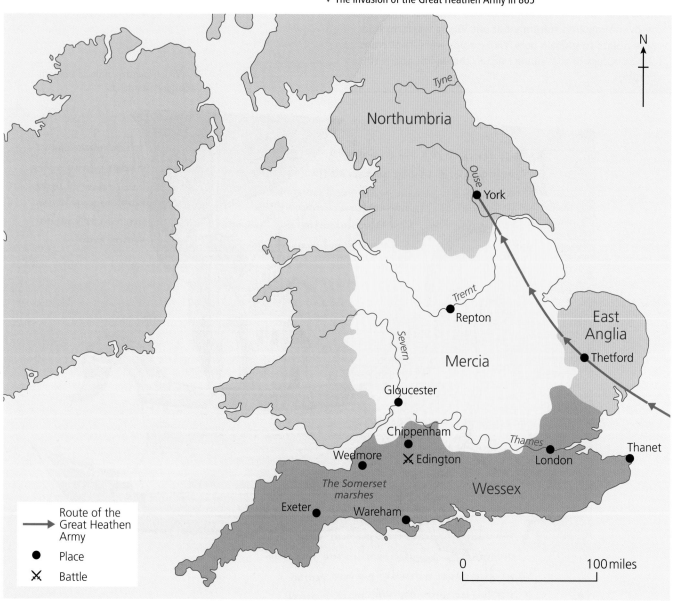

Record

The Vikings quickly gained control of England when they invaded in 865.

As you find out about the Vikings' invasion of England in 865, make a list of bullet points to challenge this over-simple statement.

The invasion of the Great Heathen Army, 865–79

865 Halfdan and Ivar the Boneless landed in East Anglia and unfurled their black raven banner at the head of the Great Heathen Army. The King of East Anglia bought them off by supplying them with horses.

866–67 From their base at Thetford, the Danes advanced north through Mercia and into Northumbria. They captured York on 1 November 866, a day when the city was packed with people celebrating All Saints Day in the cathedral. In 867 the Northumbrian king Aelle was put to death. It is said that Halfdan and Ivar performed the 'blood eagle' ritual on him (see page 53).

869 The Great Army returned to its camp at Thetford. In the autumn, the Vikings attacked the heartlands of East Anglia. They killed the East Anglian king, Edmund, and took over his kingdom.

870–71 With the southern part of Northumbria and East Anglia now under Danish control, and Mercia presenting no serious threat, the Danes turned to the Anglo-Saxon kingdom of Wessex. In 870 they crossed the River Thames at Reading and fought the West Saxons in a series of confrontations across northern Wessex. Many lives were lost on both sides, but the Vikings were unable to defeat the West Saxons.

873–74 The Great Army attacked Mercia and over-wintered at Repton, an important crossing point on the River Trent (see page 58). The Mercian king Burgred fled to Rome and the Danes seized the eastern half of his kingdom.

875 The Great Army split:

- Halfdan led one part of the army north to take full control of his kingdom in Northumbria.
- Guthrum, the leader of the other part of the army, marched south in a second attempt to conquer Wessex.

875–78 At first, Guthrum's warriors were successful. They captured the towns of Wareham, Exeter, Gloucester and Chippenham. Alfred, King of Wessex, retreated for safety to the Somerset marshes where he planned his next move against the Vikings. At Easter 878 Alfred gathered a huge force of men from Somerset, Wiltshire and Hampshire. Alfred's army defeated Guthrum's warriors at the Battle of Edington. Guthrum was baptised as a Christian, took the name Athelstan and retreated to East Anglia in 879.

Repton

In the winter of 873–74 the Great Heathen Army established a camp at Repton, on the River Trent, during their campaign against the kingdom of Mercia. Repton was the site of an important Anglo-Saxon monastery and an important place for the Mercian kings. In the 1970s archaeologists made some remarkable discoveries at Repton.

A survey of the site revealed that the Vikings had created a D-shaped enclosure by building an earth rampart next to the river. The Vikings included the monastery in their defences, probably using the church's north and south doors as the entrance to their camp.

▼ A plan of the Viking camp at Repton

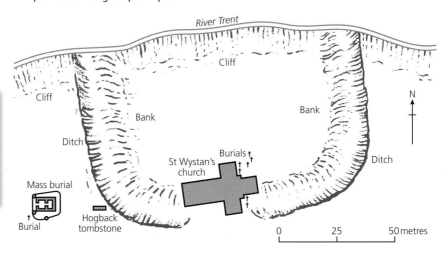

Reflect

Archaeologists cannot be certain about the reasons for the mass burial at Repton. What is your suggestion?

▼ Skeletons in the mass burial found at Repton

Archaeologists excavated a burial mound outside the defensive enclosure at Repton and were amazed by what they found: a huge collection of some 264 skeletons in a mass grave.

Analysis of the bones produced some intriguing results:

- The skeletons had been stacked up in a huge pile.
- Weapons, jewellery and coins found with the skeletons clearly showed that they were Vikings.
- Many skeletons were incomplete and some parts of the mass burial consisted of jumbled-up bones and skulls.
- 82 per cent of the bones were male, 18 per cent female.
- 68 per cent of the bones belonged to people aged 17–35, 25 per cent aged 36–45 and 5 per cent under 17.
- Many skeletons showed evidence of wounds. Of the skulls, 45 per cent of the males and 30 per cent of the females had suffered serious cuts.

The Danelaw

In 878 King Alfred of Wessex and Guthrum the Danish leader reached a peace agreement at Wedmore in Somerset. Sometime later, they made this more formal with the Treaty of Wedmore which established a line across England. This was intended to be a permanent boundary between the Saxons and the Danes.

> This is the Treaty that King Alfred and King Guthrum … have with oaths confirmed, for themselves and their descendants, as well for born as for the unborn:
>
> Concerning our land boundaries: Up on the River Thames, then up on the River Lea unto its source, then straight to Bedford, then up the River Ouse to Watling Street.

Alfred had all the area south and west of this line, extending his Kingdom of Wessex to include the western half of Mercia. The Danes ruled the area to the east and north. They were free to settle there and live according to their own laws and customs. By the eleventh century the Danish area was being called the Danelaw, because of the different legal code practised there, based on Danish law.

This map shows the division of England between Anglo-Saxon Wessex and the Danelaw. Just two generations after the raid on Lindisfarne, the Vikings held nearly half of England.

▼ The Danelaw

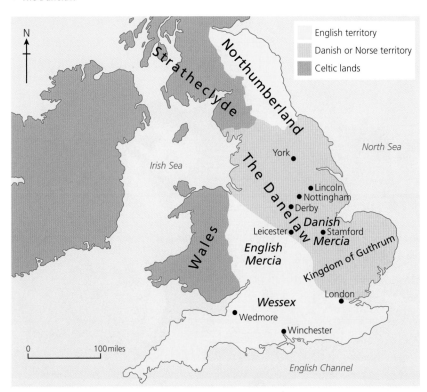

Record

Finish your list of bullet points challenging the over-simple statement that the Vikings quickly gained control of England when they invaded in 865.

Review

Use your three lists to write an essay in response to the following question:

How far do you agree that the Viking raiders of the eighth and ninth centuries were fierce warriors who easily conquered the territories of western Europe?

Images of Viking raiders

The portrayal of the Vikings as brutal raiders started with the descriptions in the Anglo-Saxon Chronicle (see page 43) and has continued into modern times. Since the nineteenth century, generations of artists and film-makers have portrayed the Vikings as ferocious warriors who brought terror to the people of western Europe.

'Slaughter on the Shore', 1890

In nineteenth-century Scandinavia there was a revival of interest in the Vikings, and artists began to imagine scenes from the Viking raids. In 1890, the Danish artist Lorenz Frølich painted this picture of a Danish attack on the monastery at Tavistock in Devon. As you can see, a big, bearded Viking wearing a stolen bishop's mitre, carries a girl off into slavery and forces a monk to bring loot from the monastery. Several dead bodies lie on the ground and the monastery burns in the background.

▼ 'Vikings Plundering a Monastery', a painting by Lorenz Frølich, 1883

Reflect

The three images on these pages are examples of the ways in which artists and film-makers have portrayed the Viking raiders. Take a closer look and analyse the images:

● How exactly are the Viking raiders portrayed?
● What similarities and differences can you find between the images?
● How do you account for these?

The Viking attack on the Irish monastery of Clonmacnoise

Tom Lovell was a famous American illustrator and painter from the twentieth century. He produced many historical illustrations for the *National Geographic Magazine,* including a series of images depicting the conquests of the Vikings. Lovell did careful historical research in order to produce what he considered to be accurate depictions of Viking raids. In this illustration he depicts the Viking raid on the Irish monastery of Clonmacnoise.

▶ A modern illustration of the Viking attack on the Irish monastery of Clonmacnoise by the American illustrator and painter Tom Lovell

A scene from the TV series *The Vikings*

The Vikings is a historical drama series shown on the TV channel 'History'. It is written and created by the English screenwriter and producer Michael Hirst. The first series was shown in 2013 and became very popular. A fifth series of twenty episodes was screened in 2016. The series was inspired by the saga of the Viking chieftain Ragnar Lothbrok who became powerful through his successful raids on England. The image below is a still from the series and shows a Viking raid in England.

▼ From *The Vikings* (2013–16), on the TV channel 'History'

4

Settlers in the west

How did the Viking settlements vary?

▲ The Settlement Exhibition in Reykjavik, Iceland. The remains of the early Viking longhouse were found when a hotel was about to be built. The special basement was created below the hotel to preserve the precious remains and allow the public to see them

This must be one of the world's most curious museum exhibitions. It is found in a very expensive, purpose-built basement below a modern hotel block in Reykjavik, the capital city of Iceland.

At the centre of the exhibition are the stone remains of a tenth-century Viking longhouse, believed to be the home of some of the very first Vikings to settle in Iceland. This photograph shows these remains under spotlights, with a mock fire in the hearth where a real one would have burned ten centuries ago.

Around the longhouse, the museum has used all sorts of modern techniques to give a sense of life at the site in the past:

- Electronic screens on the walls show visitors the view of the coastline and landscape that the original Viking settlers would have seen.
- Video animations appear on the screens to show how those first settlers lived.
- Touch-screen, computerised displays allow visitors to learn more about the objects found on the site and to explore a 3D virtual reconstruction of the longhouse itself.

It is a remarkable interpretation of a Viking settlement. But this was just one such settlement. Between 800 and 1000, Vikings moved westwards from Scandinavia and made new homes on the fringes of western Europe and far out across the North Atlantic. The map on page 63 gives an overview of this extraordinary movement and shows where and when Vikings settled in the west.

▼ Viking settlements in the west, c. 800–c. 1000. Dates show when the first significant settlements were established in each place

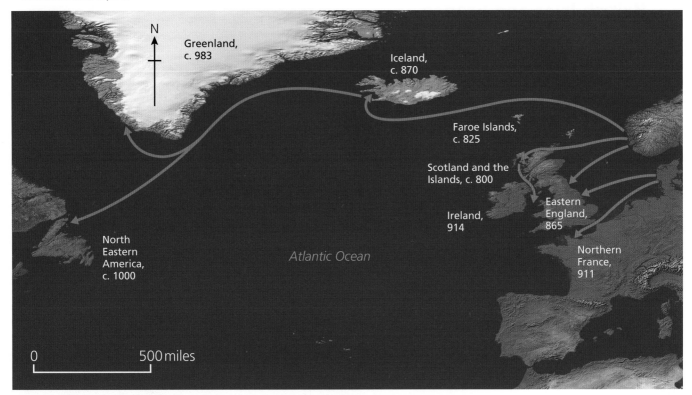

The Enquiry

As you learned in Enquiry 3, Vikings first appeared in the west as traders or as raiding warriors who returned home after gaining what they wanted. In this enquiry, however, you will learn how some Vikings became settlers, making new homes in lands far from Scandinavia.

You will learn about:

- Viking settlement in the British Isles and France
- Viking life in Jorvik (York)
- Viking settlement across the Atlantic, in Iceland, Greenland and North America

As you work through the enquiry, you will draft the text for a series of eight information screens that could be used on a touch-operated display at a museum like the one in Reykjavik.

For each of your eight screens you must:

1 Write a clear and organised summary that analyses:
   a **Settlement** – how the Vikings lived in that place, e.g. in towns or in the countryside
   b **Social integration** – how far the Vikings mixed with any people already living in the new lands
   c **Political structures** – how the Vikings ruled themselves and others in the area
2 For each screen, you must also select one image to accompany the summary and explain how your selected image will help the touch-screen viewer to understand that particular settlement.

Viking settlement in the British Isles and France

Viking settlement in the west started in the lands across the North Sea that were closest to the Vikings' Scandinavian homelands.

Scotland and the islands

With very few written records to help them, historians rely heavily on archaeology and other non-documentary evidence to reveal where and when the Vikings chose to settle down in these new lands.

Burials and beliefs

Among the best evidence for Viking settlement in and around Scotland are burial sites. By examining bones and other objects found in these Viking burials, historians have calculated that the settlements were made as follows:

- The Shetlands and Orkneys, around 800
- The far north east coast of the Scottish mainland, before 825
- The west coast and the Hebrides islands, by 825
- The Isle of Man, by 850

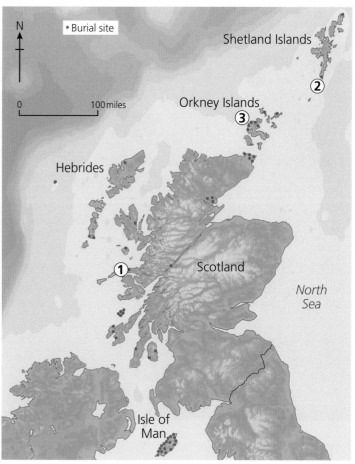

▲ Viking burial sites in Scotland and the islands

Many of these burials suggest that the Vikings who settled in this region still followed their own pagan beliefs. In 2011, a Viking boat-burial (see page 23) was excavated at Ardnamurchan, the most westerly point of the Scottish mainland (point 1 on the map). It has been dated to the early tenth century. The timbers of the vessel had almost entirely rotted away but its outline and around 200 rivets still remained in place. The mourners had dragged the boat up the beach to higher ground, propped it up and filled it with stones before adding grave goods to support the dead man in the next life. These included a shield and weapons and suggest that he was a man of high status. Archaeologists believe that the place where he was buried was a particularly special site to the Picts who inhabited the region when the Vikings arrived. Some see this as a sign that the Vikings were eager to adopt some of the local customs.

By 1000, Vikings had converted to Christianity and from that time it is more difficult to tell from graves whether the person buried was of Viking origin. On the Isle of Man, however, graves have been found that are marked by large stone slabs that show the Christian cross as well as figures from Viking mythology, such as the god Odin. This is evidence of the gradual move from pagan Norse beliefs to the Christianity followed in the British Isles at that time.

▶ A tenth-century Viking cross slab from the Isle of Man. The timber shows parts of the cross that have disappeared. Alongside the cross, stands Odin with one of his messenger ravens and spear, as he is attacked by a wolf

Buildings

Most remains of Viking settlements in the far north are on sites that were previously inhabited by Picts, the tribe that lived in Scotland before the Vikings arrived. These sites are all beside the sea as ships provided links to other islands and back to Norway. But they also had fresh water and good land that supported farming.

The largest set of Viking farmhouses anywhere in Britain has been found at Jarlshof on Shetland (point 2 on the map). It is far too small to be called a town and is barely a village. Other remains on the same site date back many centuries before the Vikings arrived. This implies that the Vikings were taking over a small but well-established settlement. Finds in Viking rubbish pits, known as middens, reveal that they continued to trade widely, ate a lot of fish and also farmed the land, keeping animals and growing crops.

▲ The largest of the Viking longhouses found at Jarlshof in the Shetland Isles. This Viking farm settlement dates to some time in the ninth century. Stone was used for walls as it was more readily available than timber

Reflect

What sorts of finds in middens would tell archaeologists that the Vikings farmed and fished for their food and also traded widely?

Viking power and control

At first, local chiefs ruled different Viking settlements but by 1000, the kings of Norway had set up an Earldom of the Orkneys that covered the Shetlands and the Orkneys, and a Kingdom of the Isles that included the Hebrides and the Isle of Man. From 1014 to 1065, the Earl of the Orkneys was Thorfinn the Mighty who ruled from a settlement at Birsay (point 3 on the map). On a nearby island, archaeologists have uncovered what may be part of the remains of Thorfinn's base. Even such an important site was never large enough to be called a town. The Vikings in and around Scotland lived in much smaller settlements.

Historians disagree about whether the Vikings completely wiped out the Picts and took their lands or whether they simply settled and lived alongside them. The Shetlands and Orkneys were almost completely dominated by the Vikings, who brought their wives and families from Norway. Until the eighteenth century, some people in these islands spoke their own language, Norn, which was similar to Norwegian. All the place names on these islands are of Norse origin. They often end in -ness, meaning a headland, or -wick, meaning a bay or inlet; Wick is the word from which Viking comes.

Similar place names dominate the Hebrides and are also common in the Isle of Man. Another important clue in place names is -ting or -ding. This is often a sign of a meeting place where Vikings assembled to agree laws and hold trials. On the Isle of Man, which still governs many of its own affairs, the parliament is still called the 'Tynwald', which means 'meeting field'.

DNA testing has shown that about 40 per cent of Shetlanders and 50 per cent of Orkney inhabitants have male Scandinavian ancestors. On the Isle of Man, the proportion is around 39 per cent. In areas of Britain where we believe there was no direct Viking settlement, the figure is between 10 and 20 per cent.

Record

Prepare your first touch-screen display as described on page 63. Use the heading **'Viking settlement in Scotland and the islands'**.

England

At the end of the last enquiry (page 59) you learned about the peace agreement made in 878 between King Alfred of Wessex and Guthrum, the Danish leader of the Great Heathen Army. This created the Viking-held region that came to be called the Danelaw. As early as 876, however, the Anglo Saxon Chronicle described how, in the east of England:

> the Danes settled, shared out the land and proceeded to plough and support themselves.

Danelaw and Danish rule

Although the Danes held this region securely for less than 50 years from 878 to 927, they had a lasting impact. Even after regaining control of the Danelaw, Anglo-Saxon kings allowed certain Danish customs to continue and even spread some throughout the rest of their kingdom. A central part of our legal system today, trial by a jury of twelve citizens, derives from the Scandinavian assemblies, the *things* described in Enquiry 1.

Danelaw was divided among different Danish jarls who each ruled a large region. They were based in *burhs* (fortified towns) and their armies were the main decision-making bodies. These *burhs* all existed before the Vikings arrived but the Danes developed some by improving their defences and their trading links. You will learn more about their settlement at Jorvik (York) on pages 70–73.

Most Viking immigrants probably lived in rural areas, farming the land. Some historians believe that Danish lords allowed the peasant farmers greater freedom than they would have had in the rest of England. When William the Conqueror carried out his Domesday survey of 1086, there was a far higher proportion of freemen in the Danelaw region than in other parts of England.

Language

Although the Vikings' language never had as much effect on England as it had on Scotland and the islands, it still left its mark. Distinctive Scandinavian patterns often appear at the ends of place names. For example:

- -by = village, as in Whitby
- -thorpe = new village, as in Hilderthorpe
- -thwaite = meadow, as in Slaithwaite
- -toft = a house, as in Lowestoft
- -ness = a headland, as in Skegness

Large numbers of place names with these endings can be found all over what was the Danelaw. In many cases this might show that Scandinavian people settled in these places but in others it may just show how Scandinavian terms were adopted by Anglo-Saxons. Either way, the Viking settlement of England clearly had a significant impact.

Given that much of the Danelaw included most of England's uplands, it is not surprising that quite a number of mountain words are of Scandinavian origin, including 'fell' (a hill), 'beck' (a stream) and 'tarn' (a small mountain lake).

The red shading on the map below shows where these place names are to be found. You can see that, in England, they nearly all coincide with the area of the Danelaw, usually where the land is fertile. There are many other commonly used words in English today that are Scandinavian in origin. They include words such as 'slaughter' and 'ransack' as well as many that are more linked to daily life: 'husband', 'sister', 'marriage', 'egg', 'window', 'sky', 'take', 'knife', 'skin', 'anger', 'birth', 'leg' and many more.

▼ Areas where place names with Scandinavian origins are commonly found

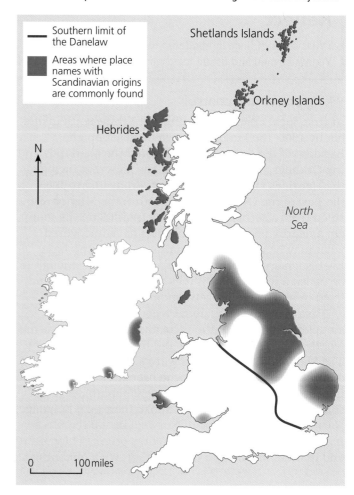

'Invisible Vikings'

Thousands of migrants from Scandinavia, mainly Denmark, followed the Great Heathen Army to England. The lands they came to were, of course, already inhabited by Anglo-Saxons. We cannot be sure how many came or how soon they began to intermarry with the locals and become absorbed into the population. It may have varied in different parts of the Danelaw, but their arrival can still be detected today. Genetic research into the DNA of people living in what was the Danelaw has found a high correlation with Scandinavian origins. Despite this, it is curiously hard to find actual physical evidence of Viking culture in England. One historian, Dawn Hadley, even calls the Danes in Danelaw 'Invisible Vikings'. The Vikings have, however, left some remarkable signs of their lives in England. A few are shown below.

▼ Tenth-century grave-markers from Yorkshire

The strange tomb monuments or grave-markers shown here can be seen in a church in the village of Brompton in North Yorkshire. Their shape resembles the curve of a pig's spine so they are known as 'hogback' tombs. There are over 100 similar stones in Britain, all in places where Vikings settled.

Vikings in Scandinavia had no tradition of making sculptured tombstones so they were obviously trying to adapt to what was an established Anglo-Saxon custom. The sides feature typical Viking-style carving and the creatures at each end are bears. They seem to be muzzled. Some historians believe the Vikings did this to show that their days of violence were over and that they had become peaceful settlers in the area. Surprisingly, many of these Viking tombs are found in villages with Anglo-Saxon names.

Hoards of Viking silver are still found in England. They often contain the coins that Guthrum started to mint, basing them on Alfred's coin designs. Coins were not in common use in Scandinavia until well into the tenth century and Vikings still loved to store their wealth as jewellery and as 'hacksilver', solid bars from which small amounts could be cut when needed.

This photograph shows a tiny part of the Cuerdale Hoard, the largest collection of Viking silver ever found in western Europe. It was made up of over 8,000 silver items and was unearthed in 1840 at Cuerdale in Lancashire.

▲ Silver objects dating from 905–10 from the Cuerdale Hoard

Simple brooches in the Viking style, as shown on page 13, are a much more humble sign of the spread of the so-called 'Invisible Vikings'. With the rise of metal-detecting as a hobby, hundreds of these brooches have been found in the ground all over the Danelaw region. Very few are found in the Anglo-Saxon parts of England. The brooches follow the basic Viking style but have Anglo-Saxon features as well. They may have belonged to women with Scandinavian origins or they may have simply become popular with Anglo-Saxons.

A pair of late ninth-century Viking style brooches, found in Suffolk ▲

Record

Prepare your next touch-screen display as described on page 63. Use the heading '**Viking settlement in England**'.

Ireland

When you learned about the Cuerdale Hoard on page 67, you may have wondered why such a treasure was found in that particular place. We don't really know the answer, but there are some clues. The latest coin in the hoard was from around 905, so we can date the hoard as no earlier, but soon after that date. At that time, Viking rulers in Jorvik were in close contact with Dublin, which became a major Viking base after their first raids on eastern Ireland in around 837. Cuerdale lies in the valley of the River Ribble, near Preston, in Lancashire, on a direct route between the two towns (see map).

In 902 the Vikings were expelled from Ireland for some years. Perhaps the Cuerdale Hoard belonged to a wealthy Irish Viking chief on the run. Or perhaps this was war-chest to pay warriors to attack and re-capture Dublin.

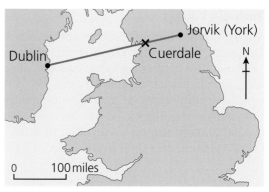

▲ The Dublin–Jorvik trade route

Dublin

In 914, Viking armies re-occupied their trading bases at Dublin, Wexford and Waterford. Archaeological excavations in modern Dublin have found well-preserved remains of rectangular, thatched Viking houses. These were made from timber posts with wattle walls covered in a mix of mud and dung.

The houses were packed closely together within strong earthwork defences that protected the port from attack. Below is an artist's impression of Viking Dublin in the tenth century: a trading port with a surrounding wall and ships drawn up on the beach. These ships were often loaded with slaves. They would have been captured on raids inland, or in battles against Irish chiefs, and then sold abroad.

▼ An artist's reconstruction of tenth-century Dublin

The interior

The absence of Viking place names suggests that few Vikings ever moved into the interior of Ireland. (See the place-name map on page 66.) The local chieftains resisted any attempt at a Viking conquest but were happy to sell their captured enemies to the Vikings as slaves.

Archaeologists have also noticed an increase in the number of sheep bones found in the Irish interior at this time and believe that the Viking demand for wool stimulated sheep farming. Just occasionally a fine Viking-made sword or an unusual find such as this games board (right) appears in an archaeological dig many miles inland. Historians believe that Irish men and women may even have travelled to Dublin to buy such special objects and show them off at home.

Gradually the Vikings became part of Irish life. They converted to Christianity, intermarried and became Gaelic-speakers. Traditionally, the Vikings were said to have been finally defeated and expelled from Ireland at the battle of Clontarf in 1014. However, by then they had really lost their Viking identity.

▼ A tenth-century Viking board game

Record

Prepare your next touch-screen display as described on page 63. Use the heading '**Viking settlement in Ireland**'.

France

As you learned on page 49, France suffered waves of Viking raids from about 800. These continued to about 930 and started again in the 980s. With one notable exception, none of these raids led to significant settlement in France. The exception came in 911, when the French King, Charles the Simple, defeated a Viking leader called Rollo in battle. He then offered Rollo lands in northern France including the town of Rouen and the mouth of the River Seine. In return for this land, Rollo promised to become Christian, to be loyal to Charles and to guard the Seine against any further Viking raids. Rollo and his successors expanded Normandy westwards, as shown by the shading on the map. First they took the lands around Bayeux in 924 and then the Cotentin peninsular in 933.

The area quickly became known as Normandy, the land of northmen.

▲ Place names of Scandinavian origin in Normandy

Numbers

The red dots on the map are places with Scandinavian names. They are mainly small settlements, near the coast and along the larger rivers. This suggests that there was relatively little colonisation by Danes further inland. Finds of Viking artefacts are very rare and so it seems that fewer Vikings settled in Normandy than in the English Danelaw. When scientists carried out DNA testing of people in Normandy in 2016, they found far less evidence of Viking ancestry than is the case in the Scottish islands or even the east of Britain.

From Vikings to Normans

Historians believe that the Vikings who settled in Normandy quickly took on a French identity. They married into local families and became French-speakers, leaving far less impact on the language or place names than was the case in Britain. They also became deeply committed to Christianity and by 1050 the Church in Normandy was particularly strong. Vikings also adopted the French form of warfare that relied heavily on knights (well-trained warriors who fought on horseback).

Although the Dukes of Normandy kept some cultural links with their forefathers' Viking ways of life, the last Norwegian *skald* (poet) performed at the Norman court in 1025. Trade with Scandinavia also declined as the Viking settlers in Normandy developed links with England and the rest of western Europe. When Rollo's descendant Duke William invaded England and took the crown by his victory at Hastings in 1066, he did so as a French-speaking Norman, a 'Northman' in name only.

▲ A nineteenth-century statue of William the Conqueror in Falaise, France. The figures around the base are his Viking ancestors. Rollo is at the front corner

Record

Prepare your next touch-screen display as described on page 63. Use the heading '**Viking settlement in France**'.

Viking life in Jorvik (York)

Record

As you read pages 70–73, find ideas and information to include in your next touch-screen summary. It will be called **'The Viking settlement in Jorvik – a case study of town life'**.

The city of York has played an important role in the life of northern England for over 2,000 years. The Romans called it Eboracum and made it an important army base, fortified with walls. Under the Anglo-Saxons it was called Eoforwic and was the capital of the kingdom of Northumbria and an important Christian centre. In this aerial photograph, you can see the cathedral, York Minster, standing in the area outlined in red. This was the area of the city first developed by the Romans.

▲ The city of York today. The red line shows the old Roman city now dominated by the cathedral, York Minster. The yellow lines show the area of the Coppergate dig within the part of the city developed later by the Vikings

The Vikings of the Great Heathen Army captured the city from the Anglo-Saxons in 866 and called it Jorvik. It was fought over and changed hands several times in the next century but, as the leading town of Danelaw, Jorvik flourished. The Vikings added new streets on both sides of the river in the area in the lower half of the photograph. By the year 1000, Jorvik had a population of about 10,000 and was one of the most important cities in northern Europe.

Streets and layout

The Vikings added new streets to the older Roman and Anglo-Saxon town. Most of these new streets were close to the banks of the River Ouse, which was deep enough to allow sea-going ships to sail through the marshes and into Jorvik. This was a large port that linked the northern half of Danelaw with the wider world, especially back to Scandinavia.

Some historians believe that the organised street layout and the similar size and design of the houses that have been excavated at Jorvik suggest that the development was carefully controlled by the town's rulers. Even if it was planned with some care, a Viking saga describes Jorvik as dark and dank.

Many of modern York's street names date back to the Viking Age. They give clues about what went on in that area of the town. They often end in '-gate' from the Viking word for a street:

- Skeldergate – Shield-maker Street
- Hungate – Hounds Street
- Swinegate – Pig Street
- King's Staith – King's quay (a landing place)

Another street in Viking times was called Brettegate. It was beyond the town walls and was the area where 'Britons' lived. These Britons were Celtic people from Cumbria and were brought to Jorvik by Vikings from Dublin. It is likely that they were used as labourers and were given their own, separate area in which to live. This was not the case for Anglo-Saxons who seem to have carried on living alongside migrants from Scandinavia inside the walls of Jorvik.

The Coppergate dig

Archaeologists have carried out digs at a number of sites across York. The largest and most interesting of these for finding out about Viking Jorvik was at a street named Coppergate that was investigated between 1976 and 1981.

An old sweet-making factory was demolished and, before a new shopping centre was built on the site, archaeologists excavated an area of about 1,000 square metres. (It is marked in yellow on the photograph on page 70.) The unusually wet earth close to the river had preserved over 20,000 objects and structures that threw light on the lives of the people who had lived in Jorvik during the period 866–c. 1050.

Only one human burial was found at the Coppergate dig but many skeletons from the Viking period have been found in a nearby church cemetery. From these, historians have discovered that:

- few people lived for more than 60 years
- a quarter of all people died in childhood
- a half of all women died by the age of 35.

The fact that these bodies were buried in a churchyard strongly suggests that the Vikings converted to Christianity soon after moving to England. Several of the churches that still stand in modern York were first built in Viking times. These include St Olave's which was founded in c. 1055 and is dedicated to a Scandinavian saint.

▲ The Coppergate archaeological dig in York, c. 1980

Coppergate homes and workplaces

The houses excavated at Coppergate were tightly packed and windowless, very similar to those discovered at excavations in Dublin. They were timber-built and of uniform size, measuring 7 metres long by 4.5 metres wide. Some had a little yard outside with a latrine, and some later ones had low cellars for storage. Woven wattles were used to make walls, pathways and screens.

The name Coppergate means 'Cup-maker Street' and among the finds discovered there were many wooden cups, plates and bowls. They had been turned on a lathe. The cups were for drinking beer, the normal Jorvik drink. These and all the other evidence found in Coppergate suggest that it had been a street of craftspeople of many kinds, making things from wood, metal, leather, bone and other materials.

While Scandinavian styles did affect the shapes of objects such as pots used for cooking and brooches worn to fasten clothing, very little evidence was found at Coppergate to suggest that Jorvik was an exclusively Viking town. It seems likely that the Viking settlers lived in a very similar way to the Anglo-Saxons around them. The two groups probably intermarried from an early stage and lived alongside each other throughout the town.

▲ Some of the many wooden bowls, plates and cups found at Coppergate in c. 1980

Reflect

What sorts of objects do you think archaeologists might find in each of the streets listed on page 70?

Trading links

Evidence from Jorvik shows many signs of the Vikings' extensive trading links. Excavations in the tenth-century Anglo-Saxon port of Hamwic (now Southampton) show similar objects but its trading links were more limited.

Reindeer antler was brought from the Arctic and was cut and shaped by specialist antler- and bone-carvers in Coppergate. They made all kinds of items such as pins, strap-ends, rings and amulets. Hundreds of combs were found. Most, like this one had teeth made of antler, held in place by a bone frame, sometimes decorated. A comb was an important, prized personal possession for a Viking, not only for dealing with long hair, but for getting rid of lice. Some of the excavated combs still had the fossilised remains of head-lice attached.

Walrus ivory from the Arctic regions was an expensive luxury so it was surprising to find that a lump had been carved into a six-sided die, used for games and gambling.

Special stones were imported from Scandinavia and Germany to make high quality querns, which were used for grinding grain, and smooth-sided moulds for metalwork.

Leather shoes of different styles were found. There were several shoemakers in Coppergate as well as craftspeople making other leather items such as belts, pouches and scabbards. The leather came from animals that had been caught and butchered locally, although the shoe on the left in this photograph is of a style unknown anywhere in Britain. It may have been worn by a foreign trader visiting Jorvik.

All kinds of **metals** were worked in Coppergate. Metals found included gold and silver from Europe or Ireland, copper and lead from the Pennine range, and tin from Cornwall. A blacksmith might work with 'bog iron' dug up from the moors nearby but some higher quality metals came from Scandinavia or Germany. The goods produced included tools, ornaments and even padlocks.

Amber from Scandinavia was found in several houses at Coppergate. Often it had been carved into pendants that were strung on cords with glass beads to make necklaces.

A single, small **cowrie shell** was also found. These come from Arabia. It had been brought thousands of miles to Jorvik.

So too had the **silk** from which this cap was made. The ribbons that would have fastened below the chin have rotted away and any colours have faded, but the silk cap itself has survived. It was found with offcuts of silk in a Coppergate workshop. The nearest suppliers of silk were in Constantinople. Only a person of high status and considerable wealth could have afforded to buy a cap like this.

Reflect

Which of the objects mentioned above do you think best sums up important aspects of life in Jorvik?

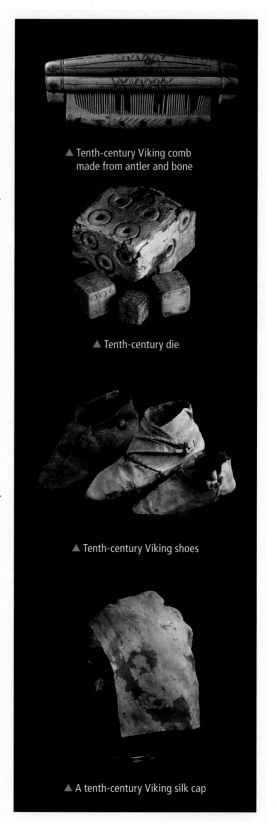

▲ Tenth-century Viking comb made from antler and bone

▲ Tenth-century die

▲ Tenth-century Viking shoes

▲ A tenth-century Viking silk cap

Kings

Among the finds at Jorvik were many coins. These help us to identify the Viking warrior kings who used Jorvik as their base. From this capital they ruled their lands in the north of England. It had an unsettled history:

- **866–927** – There were eleven Viking or Viking-controlled rulers, many of whom had close links with Dublin.
- **927–39** – The town was brought back under Anglo-Saxon control by Athelstan, King of Wessex, who expelled the Vikings from most of England.
- **939** – Olaf Guthfrithsson, King of Dublin, regained Jorvik.
- **954** – Eric Bloodaxe (who may have ruled Norway for a short period) was driven out of Jorvik. The town as well as the Viking lands it controlled once again became part of the Kingdom of England.
- **After 954** – Jorvik became York and was ruled by an earl who was always appointed by the English king. Some earls had Scandinavian origins.

Reflect

Jorvik was under direct Viking rule for under a century but in that time it developed a strong and distinctive Viking character. Why do you think this was?

Coins and control

As you learned on page 67, Viking kings started to mint coins in the English style when they became rulers in Danelaw. It was an early sign of how they accepted Anglo-Saxon ways. There was a very productive mint at Jorvik that produced thousands of the coins that were found in the Cuerdale Hoard. Pack-horses followed land routes across the Pennine hills to the rivers of north west England. These linked Jorvik with the Isle of Man and Dublin. The place-names map on page 66 shows how Viking settlements developed inland along these routes.

Coins provide our best evidence about the power of the Viking kings of Jorvik but historians disagree over what they tell us. Although most of the coins follow the English pattern on at least one side and include a Christian cross, the other side often shows Viking emblems such as a sword or the hammer of the god Thor. This one was minted in Jorvik in the brief reign of Olaf Guthfrithsson. It shows a raven, bird companion of the Viking god Odin. Some historians say that this shows that the Vikings were not deeply converted to Christianity and that they lived and ruled as pagans. Only one Viking ruler of Jorvik was buried in the Minster but others may well have died elsewhere, so it is hard to know whether they had Christian burials.

For several years when the Vikings ruled Jorvik, coins were issued in the name of St Peter, the patron saint of York Minster. This has led some historians to say that it was probably the Archbishops and senior church leaders at the Minster who really ran the city rather than the warrior kings. It seems likely that responsibilities were shared between the Church and the kings.

▼ A tenth-century Viking coin

Record

Prepare your next touch-screen display as described on page 63. Use the heading '**The Viking settlement in Jorvik – a case study of town life**'.

Viking settlement across the Atlantic

This photograph shows what the map on page 63 cannot show: the North Atlantic Ocean is a hostile place, with wild, freezing storms and the ever-present danger of icebergs. Despite this, the Vikings made journeys across this formidable ocean to settle in the Faroe Islands, Iceland, Greenland, Newfoundland (just off the coast of North America) and possibly on the American mainland itself.

The distances are enormous: Iceland is 900 miles from Norway and Greenland is another 800 miles from Iceland. Settling in these lands must rank among the most impressive of all the Vikings' achievements.

▲ A storm in the North Atlantic Ocean

The Viking explorations and settlements across the North Atlantic were part of the much wider expansion of Scandinavian people that you have been learning about in this enquiry. Many of the settlers in the lands in the North Atlantic left Norway because they wanted what Norway never had enough of: usable land. Although the islands of the North Atlantic were bleak and their winters cold, they had plenty of good grazing land which, because the islands were virtually uninhabited, belonged to no one and was there to be occupied.

The sagas, however, tell a different story. They say that that the Norwegian jarls who led these expeditions resented the growing power of Harold Fairhair, the first ever King of all Norway and headed off to live the independent lives they loved. But the dates don't quite fit that story: Harold Fairhair ruled from about 872 and we know that the first Vikings settled in Iceland from about 870.

Reflect

What two reasons are given for the Viking settlement of lands in the North Atlantic?

Even before they reached Iceland, the Vikings had settled on the Faroe Islands, about 190 miles north-west of Scotland. Irish monks had lived on the islands since about 700, but Vikings arriving from Scotland or Ireland drove them away around 825. Over time, settlers from Norway brought animals to graze the land, built houses and started a community that has lived there ever since. But this was just the first step in the Viking expansion into the North Atlantic.

Iceland

The sagas tell us that the first Viking to see Iceland was Gardar the Swede, blown off course on a voyage from Scotland to the Faroes in about 860. Soon afterwards, Floki Vilgerdarson set out to explore the island. He was caught by bad weather and sea-ice and was forced to spend a freezing winter there. He and his crew nearly died, but were astonished to see miles of fresh green pasture when spring came. They were probably also impressed by the large numbers of walrus along the coastline. Ivory from walrus tusks would fetch a high price in Europe and other trading centres.

First settlement

Although Floki rather discouragingly named the island 'Iceland', the first settlers were not put off and began to arrive about the year 870. The first permanent settlement was made in 874 by Ingolfr Arneson near the present capital, Reykjavik, and he was followed by many more. Just as in the Faroe Islands, it may be that Irish monks had settled in Iceland some time before the Vikings arrived. They had either already left the island or left soon after these first Vikings settled.

Recent work on the DNA of Icelanders shows that while most of the males were of Norwegian origin, with some Danes and Swedes, a high proportion of the females had come from Ireland and the Scottish islands. The animals brought to Iceland were all breeds that come from Norway. It is likely that advance groups took boat-loads of these animals to Iceland and left them there to see if they could survive the winter. People would only have followed in large numbers once they knew that they could rely on livestock for food.

Just like the sheep, pigs and cattle, settlers from north Norway would have been able to cope with the Icelandic climate but it would have been hard work. Growing cereals was difficult, but grazing stock, together with fishing and hunting, provided a basic living. All the best grazing land is by the coast, away from the harsh interior and by 930 virtually all the useful land had been settled.

It is worth thinking about what this migration involved. The photograph below shows a modern replica of a type of Viking ship called a *knarr*. It is wider than the longship described on page 24 and sits higher in the water. It has only four *rums* of oars, for manoeuvering, and is mainly a sailing ship. It was in open ships like this that migrants, with all their families, slaves and belongings, as well as horses, cattle, sheep, pigs, dogs and chickens made the journey across the North Atlantic to Iceland.

▶ Shipwrights constructing a replica Viking *knarr*, c. 1997

Houses

This is a reconstructed early settler's farmhouse in Iceland. It has walls of stone with a sod (turf) roof. Timber was so precious that it was used only for the doors and roof supports. It is possible that Iceland was wooded when the settlers arrived but once they had cut those trees down no more grew. From then on, timber had to be imported from Norway or gathered from the beaches where it had been washed up as driftwood.

The migration to Iceland was led by jarls, who arrived with their followers and occupied large tracts of land, farming some themselves and apportioning the rest to their bondi. The *Landnamabok*, compiled in about 1100, names 430 of the first leaders and lists precisely where they settled. Nearly all the settlements were near the coast, away from the barren mountains of the interior. There were no towns anywhere on Iceland until the eighteenth century. Before then, even the capital, Reykjavik, consisted of a widespread range of farm settlements.

▲ Tourists visit a modern reconstruction of a Viking farm in Iceland, c. 2010

Calculations from a census taken in 1095 gave a total population of about 50,000 at that time. The population in 2016 was still only 350,000 and the great majority of residents are directly descended from the first Viking settlers.

The *Althing*

Icelandic society recreated old Norwegian society and consisted of free farmers, about 40 chieftains (*goðar*), and no kings.

At first, as you can imagine, there were bloody quarrels between settlers over land boundaries. However, local assemblies, called *things* as they were back home in Norway, were set up to settle disputes, presided over by the *goðar*. In 930 an all-Iceland assembly, the *Althing*, met for the first time. Until 1799 it took place in the open air at Thingvellir. On page 77 you can see an artist's impression of an *Althing* taking place, as well as a recent photograph of the site as it is today.

All free men could attend the assemblies, which were usually the main social event of the year. People came from all over the island and camped out in order to attend.

The artist's depiction opposite emphasises the wild environment, the scattered groups of people and the Law-Speaker standing on the highest point. The assembly started with a recital of all the laws of Iceland by the Law-Speaker, from memory: this took two days.

Only free men could vote in the actual proceedings of the *Althing*, but this at least was more egalitarian than the monarchies being established in Scandinavia at this time (see Enquiry 5). Land disputes were settled and major decisions were taken. The most important decision came in 1000 when a great debate was held over whether or not to adopt Christianity. The *Althing* left it to the Law-Speaker to decide and, although a pagan himself, he decided that Iceland should become Christian.

▲ A late nineteenth-century painting recreating a scene at the Icelandic *Althing*. The artist is W.G. Collingwood

▶ The site of the *Althing* meeting as it is today. The photograph and painting show the site from opposite directions

Record

Prepare your next touch-screen display as described on page 63. Use the heading '**Viking settlement in Iceland**'.

Greenland

Although most of Greenland is covered with ice, the far southern tip reaches a rather warmer region, on the same latitude as the Shetlands (see the map on page 63). Vikings first settled there around 983 when a criminal called Erik the Red was banished from Iceland for three years. He had heard of a land to the west and he set out to investigate. He reached a new land but its eastern shores were ice-bound and uninhabitable. He sailed on, around the southern tip, and found that the western coast was like Norway, with long fjords reaching deep inland, bordered by good pasture for grazing.

Erik called his discovery Greenland, hoping this promising name would attract settlers. His plan worked and, in 986, he set off from Iceland to settle there with 25 ships filled with people and their livestock. Only fourteen ships made it, but soon two settlements were established on the west coast. Confusingly, the one further north became known as the Western Settlement and the one in the south became known as the Eastern Settlement. (See the map on page 79.)

▲ The ruins of *Brattahlíð* in Greenland. This was the Eastern Settlement created by Erik the Red in 986

Hunting, farming, trading

Life was tough in these Greenland settlements but the land was more fertile than in Iceland. The settlers may even have been able to grow crops as well as keeping cattle, sheep and goats. They caught fish, seals and whales from the sea and hunted bear, deer and birds on land.

The Greenlanders relied on trade with Iceland and Europe for everything else they needed. They had to import most of their timber and grain and all their metal. Barely any old iron is found in middens (rubbish tips) on Greenland: it was too precious to throw away even a nail.

Traders from Iceland and Europe were prepared to bring these things to Greenland as the settlers there had highly prized goods to sell: polar bear and arctic fox furs, falcons, seal and walrus hide for rope, whale baleen and, most precious of all, walrus tusk ivory. So many remnants of bone combs have been found that some archaeologists believe that the Greenlanders mass-produced these and sold them for use in Europe.

▲ A walrus off the coast of Greenland

Decline and disappearance

At their peak, around 1050, the Eastern Settlement (*Brattahlíð*) had about 190 farms and the Western Settlement (*Eystribyggð*) had about 90. These were scattered along the fjords and there was nothing resembling a town. At that time, there were altogether perhaps 4,000 Vikings in Greenland. Some sagas say that the Vikings traded with local tribes of Eskimo or Inuit people but as far as we know the groups never lived alongside each other. The Viking word for these people was '*skraeling*' which can be translated as barbarians. Precious Viking objects such as metal blades and nails have been found by archaeologists at Inuit settlements in northern Canada but no one knows if this is proof of trade or whether the Inuit gathered them from abandoned Viking houses once the Vikings had left Greenland. That happened sometime in the fifteenth century, after the climate began to get colder and the Vikings in Greenland found life increasingly difficult.

Record

Prepare your next touch-screen display as described on page 63. Use the heading '**Viking settlement in Greenland**'.

North America

According to the sagas, in about 1000, a Viking ship was blown off course and briefly sighted land even further west than Greenland. When this was reported to Leif Eriksson, the son of Erik the Red, he bought the ship that had made the voyage, hired some of its crew, and sailed from Greenland, hoping to benefit from a new settlement.

Vinland

The sagas record how Leif first encountered a bare land of rock and glaciers, probably Baffin Island, and then a low, forested coast, probably Labrador. But after sailing further south he wintered at a place he called Leifsbuðir. Leif claimed that the climate there was so mild that he saw grapes growing and he called the region Vinland (Wineland). If grapes did grow at the place he found, it must have been quite far south. Some historians think he may have used the name to flatter the newly discovered land, just as his father Erik had done with Greenland.

Leif and others made two more expeditions to Leifsbuðir but they failed to make a permanent settlement. Many historians view the 'Vinland' story in the sagas as fiction but archaeology has some intriguing clues that suggest it may have existed after all.

▲ Viking voyages and settlement to Greenland and Newfoundland, 983–1015

In 1960, at **L'Anse aux Meadows**, at the extreme north of the north American island of Newfoundland, archaeologists found convincing signs of a Viking settlement. These included the foundations of a house and seven other buildings and 125 artefacts. Most of these were iron nails but there was also a Viking dress pin, a glass bead and some bone needles.

There is no evidence of farming but there are strong signs of ship-repairing and metalworking in a shelter that has been reconstructed (see below). This may have been a repairs base for Viking ships sailing even further south. The archaeologists decided that the site was probably occupied by a fairly small Viking group, probably led by a single chief, who were there for less than twenty years. No other people seem to have lived in that region in Viking times.

◀ A reconstructed blacksmith shelter at L'Anse aux Meadows, c. 2015. The object at the front is a stone anvil

In 2016 a team of archaeologists discovered what may be another Viking site at **Point Rosée** in the far south west of Newfoundland. It was identified using images taken by a satellite.

When archaeologists excavated the site they found the remains of turf walls made in a typically Viking style. They also found a blackened rock where a charcoal fire had obviously been used for heating bog iron. This is exactly how Vikings prepared the iron to make tools, weapons and nails, but there is no firm evidence about when the site was occupied or by whom.

Once again, there was no sign of anyone else living in the area in Viking times. More work is needed to be sure whether and for how long Vikings settled at the site and how many were there. But the site may provide more evidence that they travelled further west and reached the mainland of North America.

Record

Prepare your final touch-screen display as described on page 63. Use the heading **'Viking settlement in North America'**.

Review

Of all the different Viking settlements you have learned about in this enquiry, which one would you advise someone to visit if they wanted to get a true sense of what Viking settlements were like?

Explain your choice carefully.

The Icelandic Sagas

The Icelandic Sagas are some 40 stories about the people of Iceland in the tenth and eleventh centuries. Although there are versions of the sagas written on old parchment, like the one in the photograph, they started life as long stories told from memory to listening Icelanders. The earliest hard copies were written down in the thirteenth and fourteenth centuries and the versions that have survived are mostly copies of copies.

Unlike most literature from the medieval period, the sagas are not written in Latin about kings and knights, but are in the local language, Icelandic, and are about ordinary people. They are exciting and eventful tales of family conflicts, sometimes over several generations, of love, honour and betrayal, revenge and brutal killings. The women in them are portrayed, within the limits imposed on them in Scandinavian society, as strong and active.

The sagas are told in a direct and simple style. They describe what people did and said, without going into their inner thoughts and without comment from the storyteller. The sagas are written down as prose, but include poetry of two different kinds:

▲ This copy of Njal's saga from about 1300 is bound in sealskin

Eddic verse

These poems tell the myths and legends of the gods and heroes of Scandinavia. They are written in very straightforward language, as for example in this account of Yggdrasil, the tree of the earth:

> Three roots there are that three ways run
> Beneath the ash-tree Yggdrasil;
> Beneath the first lives Hel,
> Beneath the second the frost-giants;
> Beneath the last are the lands of men.

Skaldic verse. Skalds were poets. They had a place at every Scandinavian court and were admired for their skill in composing verses, often improvised, in praise of the king or jarl. They were also feared for their ability to turn their wit against someone with a sarcastic turn of phrase. Skaldic verse follows complex rules: every line must include alliteration and an internal rhyme. Here is a brief Skaldic verse, in Icelandic and in a translation that attempts the almost impossible task of following the same rules in English:

> Deyr fe, deyia fraendr
> deyr sialtfr it sama
> en orðztirr deyr aldregi
> Hveim er ser goðan gedr

> Cattle die, kindred die,
> Every man is mortal,
> but the good name never dies
> of one who has done well.

◀ This illuminated manuscript copy of the *Heimskringla* saga from 1394 shows the death of Olaf Tryggvason. In fact, he probably died at sea (see page 89)

Historians take great care when using sagas as historical sources about the Viking Age. It is unclear how accurate they are. Certainly they include people who we know really lived, like Erik the Red and Olaf Tryggvason. They also refer to real places and even individual boulders in the Icelandic landscape, which are still there.

Snorri Sturlason, an important Icelander who was twice Law-Speaker in the early thirteenth century, argued that the stories in the sagas were true. He said that the versions being written down for the first time in his own lifetime were based on oral versions handed down by word of mouth from generation to generation. He also argued that the Skaldic verses were so widely known that any mistakes would be recognised at once. This may well have been true in a society that had never relied on writing as we do today.

However, the time difference between when the sagas were written down and the events they describe, at least 250 years, must cast doubt on their accuracy. Errors will have been made during copying, and versions of the stories may well have been amended and edited. Furthermore they were written down by Christian monks whose opinions and misunderstandings may have affected how accurately they recorded the lives and beliefs of pagan Icelanders.

Most of all, they were not written as history, but as entertainment – good stories to be listened to around the fire during the long Icelandic winter evenings. They would have been shaped by storytellers to be more dramatic, and elements of magic would have been added. Historians today regard them as 'historical novels': accurate in the names and places and in their portrayal of attitudes and values; less reliable in their factual details.

To Icelanders, the sagas are really important: they record their genealogy, telling them who they are. By the twentieth century the manuscripts of the sagas were in Copenhagen, Denmark. When they were returned to Iceland in 1971 aboard an Icelandic gunboat, thousands of people turned out to see them arrive.

5

Great Danes

How did Danish kings show their power, 958–1035?

▶ A tenth-century 'Harald Bluetooth cross-coin'. It was found in 2015

One day in October 2015, Robert Poulsen, a Danish cable-layer who likes to take his metal-detector with him as he digs his trenches, made an interesting find. In a small field at Omø in Denmark, he found 550 silver coins, jewellery and other silver objects. Among these was this coin, photographed seconds after it was lifted from the sandy soil in which it had lain for over a thousand years.

The coin was so thin that it didn't show up straight away on the metal detector and its design did not seem particularly impressive at first sight, but an expert soon identified it as something very special. It is known as a 'Harald Bluetooth cross-coin', so called because it was minted in the reign of the Danish King Harald Bluetooth (958–86) and because it has a cross on the back. It is very rare and very important: these were the first coins ever to be minted in Denmark and minting coins was a sign of authority and control. While it may not have registered on Robert Poulsen's metal detector, this little coin sends strong signals about the power of the king who had it made.

In Enquiry 1, you found out about the simple Scandinavian way of life at the beginning of the Viking Age, in about the year 750. At that time, powerful jarls sometimes called themselves 'kings', but they were really just war-lords. They were not kings as we usually understand them, ruling a country. Neither Denmark, Norway nor Sweden was a unified country in 750: different regions had their own laws and customs and local jarls refused to accept anyone as their overlord.

Since that time, the events you have been finding out about in Enquiries 2, 3 and 4 had changed Scandinavia. By the late tenth century, the lands of Scandinavia were being drawn together under fewer but more powerful jarls. The first region of Scandinavia to emerge with a single king was Denmark. That was Gorm the Old, but it was his son, Harald Bluetooth, who showed considerable power and firmly established the new kingdom of Denmark.

The Enquiry

Harald Bluetooth was the first of three remarkable kings who, from 958 to 1035, established and increased the size of the new kingdom of Denmark. In this enquiry you will learn about the achievements of each one. They were:

1 Harald Bluetooth
2 Harald's son, Svein Forkbeard
3 Harald's grandson, Cnut the Great

As you work through the enquiry you will need to weigh up the achievements of these three 'Great Danes'. You will do this by considering four different aspects of their power:

● **Religion**
● **War**
● **Trade**
● **Land**

You will build up a 'summary sheet' for each king. This is how the first one should look when you start.

At the top of each sheet, write the name of the king and the dates when he reigned.

Underneath the heading, on the left, draw a small copy of a coin from his reign. Beside that draw an empty circle.

Underneath these simple drawings, make notes about how the king showed his power in terms of each of the four aspects listed above.

When you finish learning about each king, you must turn the empty circle at the top into a pie chart, dividing it up to show how that king showed his power. If he showed his greatest achievements in religious affairs then you will make the religion part of the pie chart larger than the others. If he did very little in

King Harald Bluetooth, 958–986

Religion

War

Trade

Land

terms of trade, you will make that segment of the pie chart very small.

At the end you will need to review your notes and your pie charts and decide which of the 'Great Danes' was the greatest king and explain why you chose him.

Harald Bluetooth

Harald, whose nickname suggests that he had a very obvious dead tooth, was King of Denmark from 958 to 986. He was also king of part of Norway from 963 to 974. When he was about 28, he inherited the throne from his father, Gorm the Old. On becoming king, Harald wanted to honour his father's achievements and he did so at a place that was already very special to his family: the ancient site of Jelling in central Denmark.

Record

As you read pages 84–87, make your first summary sheet as described on page 83. At the top, copy the coin shown on page 82.

Jelling

This is the site of Jelling as it appears today. The most eye-catching features are probably the two mounds. At the bottom right is the North Mound and on the left is the South Mound. Between them are a church and a cemetery.

What is less obvious is that all these features stand over a stone-marked enclosure in the shape of an enormous ship. You can see part of the near side running beside the path, through the cemetery and beneath the South Mound. The photograph only shows half of the stone ship enclosure which stretches as far again in the other direction, over 350 metres in total. (We have shown part of its outline with a broken white line.)

Right at the centre of the picture, just visible in the photograph, are two large runestones in front of the church entrance.

This is a puzzling site, but it tells us a lot about Harald Bluetooth and his impact on Denmark.

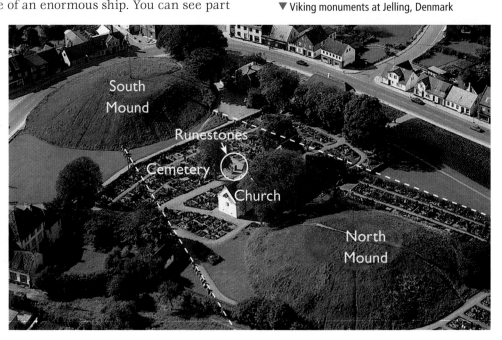

▼ Viking monuments at Jelling, Denmark

Faithful pagans

When Harald became king in 958, the site at Jelling looked very different. The great stone-marked ship dominated the scene. A small burial chamber stood on the site of the enormous North Mound. There was no South Mound at all and there was no church or cemetery, but the smaller of the two runestones was already at the site. It had been placed there by Harald's father, Gorm the Old, and its old runes explain why. They say:

> King Gorm made this monument in memory of Thyra, his wife, Denmark's adornment.

Gorm had been a pagan, believing in the Viking gods. When his wife Thyra died, Gorm chose to place a monument to her within the great stone 'ship' which, with its burial mound of an earlier Danish chief, must have been a famous pagan site at that time. Gorm was clearly proud of his pagan roots.

When Gorm died, Harald dutifully followed a similar pagan practice, burying his father in that same ship enclosure. He greatly enlarged the North Mound to the size we see today and placed his father's body there in a special chamber. Harald, like Gorm, was a proud pagan ... until he changed his mind.

Conversion to Christianity

In 965, Harald Bluetooth was baptized as a Christian. Some accounts say that a priest had impressed him with a remarkable miracle but Harald may simply have decided that it was too hard to resist the spread of Christianity. Gorm had struggled to defend Denmark against German Christian kings and if Denmark remained pagan, it would only encourage their attacks.

Christianity was already making its mark in Harald's kingdom. Missionaries from England and from Germany had been visiting Denmark since the eighth century and there were already churches in the market towns of Hedeby and Ribe. Maybe Harald felt that change was inevitable or he thought church leaders could help him rule his country. Whatever his reasons, Harald made three powerful statements at Jelling to make it known that he was now a Christian – and so were all his Danish people.

Statement 1 – The church

Harald built a wooden church exactly on the central axis of the 'ship', opposite the North Mound. A stone church later took its place but it stands on the same spot. Harald had brought Christianity right into the pagan enclosure. Over the centuries, hundreds of Christians were to be buried in its cemetery.

Statement 2 – The grave

Archaeologists have excavated the burial chamber of King Gorm and it is empty. They have also excavated the interior of the church and they have found the bones of a man who had once been buried elsewhere, along with small pieces of gold brocade from a fine costume and two silver mountings. Many historians believe that Harald had the body of his pagan father removed from the North Mound and given a Christian burial in the church.

Statement 3 – The runestone

Harald ordered that a second, even more magnificent runestone be put up at Jelling. On one side the runes declared:

> King Harald ordered this monument to be made in memory of Gorm, his father, and in memory of Thyra, his mother; that same Harald who won for himself all of Denmark and Norway and made the Danes Christian.

The other side of Harald's great stone, as shown on this copy, was carved with a Viking version of Christ on the cross: the first known portrayal of Christ in Scandinavia.

Transition

Despite Harald's boast that he 'made the Danes Christian', many continued to pray to the old Viking gods. Archaeologists know that Thor's hammer emblems were still being made and worn well into the twelfth century. Nevertheless, Harald Bluetooth's conversion did make Christianity the official Danish religion. It was a gradual and largely peaceful transition. Priests were appointed, schools were started and bishops supported royal rule. Churches were built and Christian baptisms and weddings became the normal custom. This was probably Harald Bluetooth's single most important achievement.

▲ Tenth-century runestones outside the twelfth-century church at Jelling built on the site of Harald Bluetooth's wooden church

▲ Twentieth-century copy of Harald Bluetooth's Jelling runestone

Reflect

Are you surprised that pagan beliefs continued in Denmark after Harald declared it to be a Christian kingdom?

Building the nation

Harald spent the rest of his reign trying to secure and strengthen his Christian kingdom.

Extending

Harald's great runestone at Jelling refers to 'Denmark', establishing the fact that he had finished his father's work. Between them, they had created a single new kingdom from lands that had once been ruled by many chiefs.

Harald's other claim, that he also ruled Norway, is something of an exaggeration. He exploited rivalries and weaknesses between Norwegian rulers to take the region of Vik in southern Norway in 963, but he lost it again in 974.

Connecting

During that time, Harald was convinced that he would need to keep in close contact with his new lands in Norway so he moved his capital from a site at Jelling to Roskilde, on the island of Zealand (see the map on page 87). This became the centre of royal power in Denmark for centuries. The fine wooden cathedral that Harald founded there was later rebuilt in brick. In the centuries since then, almost all Denmark's kings and queens have been buried in its vaults.

Roskilde stands on high ground above a fine, sheltered harbour. Harald chose Roskilde as the capital because of its seaways and because its central position allowed ships to move freely around the Danish mainland, its many islands and (while he held them) his lands in Norway. His commitment to improving communications also led him, in 978, to build the oldest known bridge in Scandinavia. It stood at Ravning Enge, near Jelling. It was 760 metres long, 5.5 metres wide and was made of 1,500 large oak trees. By crossing an extensive patch of marshy ground, it made travel and trade across the area much easier.

Harald's achievements in connecting his kingdom so effectively led the Danish electronics firm Ericsson to name their new 'Bluetooth' wireless device after him in 1998. He is a national hero and, like the device, he connected people's lives.

Defending

Harald did what he could to protect his kingdom. He had walls built round the three important market towns of Ribe, Hedeby and Aarhus. It was in towns like these that Harald's coins were minted as they greatly improved trade. He had to keep the towns safe from attackers, which may be why the walls were built.

Denmark's most vulnerable point of attack is where it joins the German mainland. This had long been defended by a system of ramparts that stretched for over 30 kilometres. It was called the *Danevirke*, and Harald strengthened it with a new section built in 968. Despite this, in 974 the Germans managed to beat Harald's armies and capture the valuable market town of Hedeby. In this moment of weakness, he also lost control of his lands in Norway.

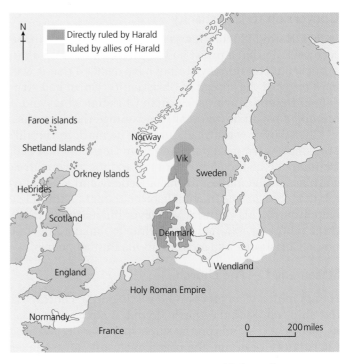

△ Lands held by Harald Bluetooth, 973

Reflect

In what ways did Harald Bluetooth try to 'connect' his lands and his people?

△ The Ericsson company's 'Bluetooth' symbol is a runic 'H' and 'B'

Dominating

This great fort at Trelleborg was built on Harald's orders. The timber foundations can be dated precisely to 980.

Just as he did with the positioning of the church at Jelling, Harald showed his concern for precision:

- The earth rampart is an exact circle, with a ditch outside.
- The gateways are at the four points of the compass.
- The two streets meet at the precise centre.
- The outlines of four identical buildings in each quarter, with more buildings outside, are carefully arranged.

There are three more forts like this across Denmark, built to the same design. The evidence suggests that the people who lived in the forts were not just soldiers but ordinary men, women and children as well. They are something of a puzzle for at least two reasons:

- An enormous amount of hard labour and materials went into preparing the ground and building the forts, yet they were occupied for only a short period and were never repaired.
- They are not in the right places to defend Denmark against invaders.

Some historians believe that Harald may have built these fortresses to show his power. He seems to have been able to call on large amounts of labour from his people – perhaps as a form of tax. Making them build fortresses of such magnificence might well have enhanced his prestige and impressed his subjects.

Other historians think they were genuine military bases, but that they were designed to subdue local chieftains and warn them against rising against Harald's royal power. Harald was only too aware that he might face resistance and rebellion at any time and these bases might have been designed to help him stabilize his country.

If that was his plan, it failed.

Defeat and death

In 985 or 986, Harald's own son Svein rose in rebellion against him and he died from wounds received in battle. As he had insisted, he was buried at Roskilde Cathedral, in the heart of his new nation, but some historians think that the South Mound at Jelling was raised as a memorial to him soon after his death.

▲ Trelleborg fortress, Denmark

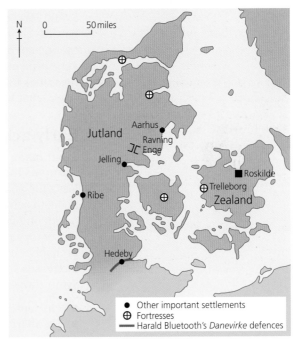

▲ Denmark c. 986

Record

Finish your first summary sheet by filling in the pie chart as described on page 83.

▲ A tenth-century coin of Svein Forkbeard

 ## Svein Forkbeard

Svein Forkbeard was the rebellious son who took the Danish throne from Harald Bluetooth in 986. His nickname suggests that he must have had a splendid long beard, splitting dramatically in two directions below the chin. It is a little disappointing, therefore, to see him on this coin with barely any sign of a beard. Around the edge, the inscription reads 'ZVEN REX AD DENER' (Sven, king of the Danes) and in the centre is a crude portrait of him with his royal sceptre.

Svein ruled Denmark from 986 to his death in 1014. He became King of most of Norway in 1000 and, in the very last few weeks of his life he became King of England.

Record

As you read pages 88–91, make your second summary sheet as described on page 83. At the top, copy the coin shown here.

One historian has described the information we have about the life of Svein Forkbeard as 'scanty and obscure'. The sagas tell us stories about his battles, but they are unreliable on details. From English sources, we know that he spent a good deal of his life attacking England, but these tell us very little about his rule in Denmark. The historian Gwyn Jones, however, describes him as 'One of the foremost Viking kings'. You will have to judge from what we know of his achievements to see if that claim is justified.

Early achievements in Denmark

Svein made his mark as a warrior in 983 when he re-captured from the Germans the important southern border town of Hedeby that had been lost nine years earlier. Two or three years later, he used the same military skills to seize the throne of Denmark from his father. He had the support of pagan chiefs who wanted to resist Harald's introduction of Christianity. After his victory he was tolerant of pagans who preferred the old ways. He also probably ended the work-tax that made Danes help to build and repair the fortresses such as the one at Trelleborg. Despite rebelling against his father, Svein showed determination to continue his father's successes.

- He continued the minting of money to support trade.
- He shared his father's belief that the Germans to the south were the greatest threat to his kingdom and expelled German bishops, fearing that they might introduce too strong a German influence.
- He boosted the growth of Christianity by inviting English Christians to help lead the Church in Denmark.
- He guaranteed the security of foreign traders, especially in the areas that were becoming more strongly Christian.

Reflect

From what you have learned so far, which do you think Svein Forkbeard was: a Christian or a pagan?

Opportunities in England

When Svein allowed his father's fortresses to fall into disrepair, he may have simply decided that Denmark was so securely under his control that they were no longer needed. He certainly seems to have been confident that all was well because, in 993 he joined forces with a Norwegian warrior called Olaf Tryggvason and sailed away with a powerful fleet to raid the coast of England. They were confident of success as Vikings from Ireland, the Isle of Man as well as Scandinavia had attacked England successfully throughout the 980s. Olaf had already attacked England in 991 and had been paid a Danegeld of 10,000 pounds of silver to leave.

An easy target

England had always been richer than Denmark, but in Svein's time it went through a period of seriously weak government. The English king, Ethelred, was only twelve at the beginning of his reign in 978. An under-age king was a problem, but his reign was also marked by treachery, cowardice, poor organisation and bad luck. Ethelred has gone down in history with the nickname 'Unready', but this is a wrong translation of the Anglo-Saxon *Unræd*, meaning 'ill-advised' or 'indecisive'.

▲ A nineteenth-century illustration of Olaf Tryggvason collecting his Danegeld

Svein and Olaf Tryggvason took full advantage of England's plight. They may have been drawn there by the fact that the supply of silver from the far east seems to have stopped in about 970 (see Enquiry 2). Svein would have wanted to ensure that silver continued to flow into Denmark – especially into the hands of the local chiefs and jarls who might otherwise turn against him.

In 993, Svein joined Olaf Tryggvason in a joint raid on England. Driven off from London, they raided Sussex and Hampshire and over-wintered at Southampton. In 994, Ethelred offered Olaf Tryggvason more money, which he took and returned to Norway, ignoring his partnership with Svein. To make matters worse, Olaf then declared himself the new King of Norway, fully knowing that Svein, as Harald Bluetooth had before him, claimed that title for himself.

> ## Reflect
>
> In the image above, how has the artist made the Vikings seem strong and the Anglo-Saxons seem weak?

New lands in Norway

When Svein returned to Denmark, he discovered that the Swedish king, Eric, had taken control there in his absence. Svein forced Eric to hand back his lands and then, when Eric died in 995, Svein married his widow, Sigrid. This was a brave move. If the sagas are to be believed, she had already murdered two other kings who had dared to propose to her. Sigrid was fiercely pagan, but this did not stop Svein from making her his wife even though he remained, nominally at least, a Christian.

This marriage was a clever political move as it created an alliance with the Swedes and made Denmark safe from any further Swedish attacks. Svein now turned on Olaf Tryggvason in Norway. With his new allies, the Swedes, he spent the next five years at war with Olaf and finally defeated him at the sea Battle of Svolder in the year 1000. Svein and the King of Sweden shared out the best Norwegian lands between them. Olaf's betrayal had backfired and Svein now had far more land in Norway than his father had ever held.

With money gained from England, new lands in Norway and an alliance with Sweden, all looked settled. But disturbing news from England in 1002 changed everything.

The turning point – massacre in England

▲ Eleventh-century skeletons found at Weymouth, Dorset in 2009

This shocking discovery was made at Weymouth in Dorset in 2009. The mass grave contained the remains of 54 broken skeletons with 51 skulls in a pile to one side.

Archaeologists examined the bones and found no sign that they had died fighting. Rather, wounds on the back of the skulls showed that they had been hacked down as they tried to escape. There were no signs of clothing, so the dead bodies must have been stripped, decapitated and tipped into their grave.

DNA testing showed that the victims were all from different regions of Scandinavia. There has been a similar find, with rather fewer people, in Oxford. It is thought that both finds are the remains from the Massacre of St Brice's Day, which took place on 13 November 1002.

On that day King Ethelred ordered a sudden surprise attack on all Danes living in England. This cannot have included all Danes in Danelaw but may have targeted groups such as mercenaries and traders in ports and towns. It was a pointless, desperate act and brought terrible revenge, opening the way for the last and most terrible period of Viking raids on England.

Reflect

What made archaeologists sure that the skeletons they found were not part of an ordinary cemetery?

King Svein's fury

Svein was enraged at this massacre of Danes. Over the next five years he returned time and again to burn and loot England:

1 **1003:** He took revenge by raiding south west England, capturing and burning Exeter, then moving on to do the same to Wilton and Salisbury.
2 **1004:** Svein attacked East Anglia, burning Norwich and Thetford.
3 **1005:** There was famine in England in 1005. No attack took place.
4 **1006–07**: Svein returned, first attacking Kent, then moving inland to ravage Hampshire. He set up a base at Reading and over-wintered on the Isle of Wight. He was bought off with 36,000 pounds of silver.

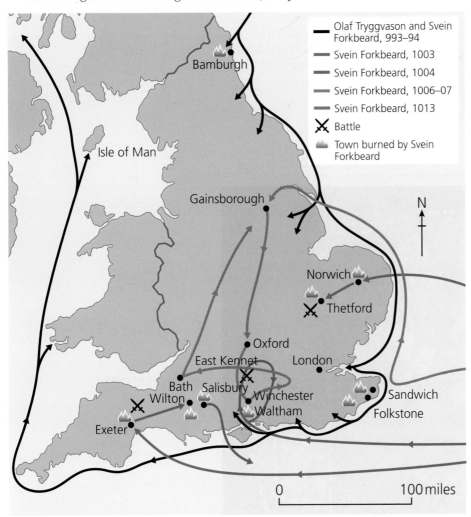

◄ Map showing Svein Forkbeard's attacks on England, 993–1013. The importance of sea-travel, the mobility it gave the Vikings and the vulnerability of England's long coastline, are all clearly demonstrated on this map

From 10,000 pounds of silver in 991, the *geld* payments rose steadily to 48,000 pounds of silver and gold in 1012. These huge amounts were made up of jewellery, church plates and coins. All this precious metal was handed over to the leaders of raiding expeditions, who then distributed it among their followers. Much of it would have been melted down to make neck-rings and other personal items and over 30,000 English coins have been found in Scandinavian graves.

Reflect

How would you describe Svein Forkbeard's character from what you have found out so far about his actions?

The treachery of Thorkell the Tall

In 1008, Ethelred tried a change of policy. He ordered the building of ships and the preparation of weapons and by 1009 a defensive fleet was ready. Unfortunately, and typically, rival commanders fell out or ran away and most of the English fleet was lost in a storm. The Viking raiders soon re-appeared and attacked the now defenceless south coast.

These Viking raids were led by Thorkell the Tall, one of Svein's most powerful Danish jarls. He raided again in 1011, burnt Canterbury and took Archbishop Aelphege prisoner. When the English failed to pay the huge ransom, the Archbishop was brutally killed in 1012 by some of Thorkell's men at a drunken feast. Thorkell then moved on to sack East Anglia and Mercia.

Later in 1012, however, Thorkell suddenly agreed to change sides and fight for Ethelred in return for the massive sum of 48,000 pounds of silver. Maybe he was recalling how the Viking warrior Rollo made a similar deal with the king of the Franks in 911 (see page 69).

Reflect

Why might the example of Rollo (see page 69) help to explain Thorkell's decision to change sides in 1012?

◀ The death of St Aelphege and other monks at Canterbury in 1012, from a thirteenth-century stained glass window in Canterbury Cathedral. The Viking murderers are shown wearing thirteenth-century armour

Reflect

Which figure in the stained glass window is Archbishop Aelphege?

The Danish Conquest, 1013

Svein was outraged that Thorkell had changed sides and that he had handed Danish ships and warriors to the English. In 1013 a huge fleet and a massive army sailed from Denmark. This time it was led by King Svein Forkbeard himself. He brought with him a professional army, not the half-Viking, half-farmer part-timers of earlier attacks. He sensed that English resistance was collapsing and the time was right for full-scale invasion and conquest.

Svein sailed first to the Kent coast, perhaps to distract Ethelred and Thorkell. But he did not land there. Instead he turned north and sailed up the Rivers Humber and Trent to make his base at Gainsborough, deep in the heart of Danelaw (see map on page 91). He was targeting the regions of England with large Danish communities. They declared him their king and so did the leaders of Northumbria. He then marched south, easily taking the key towns of Oxford, Winchester and Bath. Only London held out, defended for Ethelred by Thorkell. However, after the fall of Bath, they both fled to France to seek refuge with Ethelred's father-in-law, the Duke of Normandy. At that point even London surrendered.

On Christmas Day, 1013, without even having to fight a major battle, Svein Forkbeard became King of England.

Svein's kingdoms

Svein Forkbeard was a formidable warrior-king. If you compare this map with the one on page 86, you can see how much he had extended his lands. He looked set to develop a great empire in northern Europe. However, he became England's shortest-reigning king when he died at Gainsborough just five weeks later, on 3 February 1014. Some accounts say that he fell from his horse. His body was returned to Denmark, and he was buried in Roskilde Cathedral alongside his father, Harald Bluetooth.

Record

Finish your second summary sheet by filling in the pie chart as described on page 83.

▲ Svein and his Danish troops land in England, 1013. From a fourteenth-century manuscript. As with the stained glass window on page 92, the Vikings are shown wearing armour from the time when the picture was made

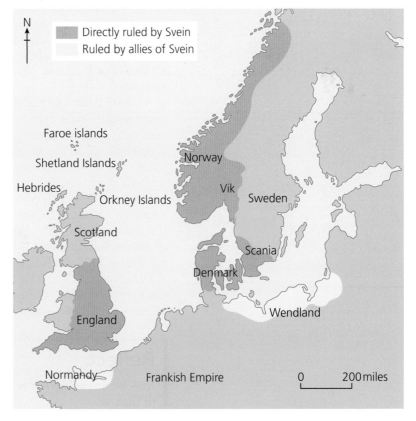

▲ Svein Forkbeard's lands at his death in 1014

Cnut the Great

This coin shows our third 'Great Dane'. It has the inscription 'CNVT REX ANGLORI' (Cnut King of the English).

Cnut ruled as King of England from 1016 until his death in 1035. By 1030 he was also King of Denmark, Norway and part of Sweden, and was Lord of the Orkneys. His fleets controlled both the North Sea and the Baltic. He had built a remarkable empire. But none of this had seemed possible when his father, Svein Forkbeard, died suddenly in February 1014. Cnut was then only eighteen years old and found himself in a terrible situation.

▲ A coin of King Cnut, minted in 1027 in London

Record

As you read pages 92–95, make your final summary sheet as described on page 83. At the top, copy the coin shown here.

Winning back the English crown

On Svein's death in 1014, the English earls and bishops rapidly recalled Ethelred from Normandy to be their king. Cnut had been fighting alongside his father in England but was now forced to return to Denmark. He had expected to become king of Denmark like his father but found that his brother Harald had already taken the throne. Within months of his father's death, Cnut was having to decide which kingdom to fight for: Denmark or England. Not surprisingly, Harald encouraged him to attack England.

By 1015 Cnut had put together a sizeable army and a large fleet. The sagas usually only count armies by the number of ships, but as we have seen, ships can be of different sizes, the largest carrying between 80 and 100 people. If, as the sagas say, Cnut set sail with 160 ships, his army must have numbered somewhere between 7,000 and 10,000 men.

Cnut made landfall at Sandwich, in Kent, then over-wintered in Poole harbour on the south coast. In 1016 he fought a series of battles across southern England. In April, Ethelred died and was succeeded by his able son, Edmund Ironside. Eventually Cnut defeated Edmund at the battle of Ashingdon, in Essex. The Anglo-Saxon Chronicle records that 'All the nobility of England was there destroyed'. They made a peace agreement at Deerhurst in Gloucestershire by which Cnut took all England north of the River Thames. Edmund held Wessex, but died only a few weeks later; by the end of 1016 Cnut was king of all England.

Reflect

How far do you think it was luck that allowed Cnut to take the throne of England?

Taking control

After so many years of raids and war, what England needed most was peace, and Cnut provided it. But some of his methods were very severe:

- He created a fleet of 40 ships to defend the country against further Viking raids. His fleet drove off 30 Viking ships in 1018.
- He raised a standing army (the housecarls) to defend the country and help him crush any rebels. They were drawn from across Scandinavia and came as mercenaries, serving as soldiers purely for the money.
- He raised the money he needed to pay for the fleet and army through a geld (tax) on the Anglo-Saxons. In 1018 alone this raised £72,000 with an additional £10,000 from London.
- He ruthlessly executed some Anglo-Saxon leaders. He took Wessex for himself and divided the rest of England into four parts, more or less along the lines of the former Anglo-Saxon kingdoms (see page 56).
- He replaced Anglo-Saxon leaders and gave their land to Danish jarls creating an Anglo-Danish aristocracy. However, there was no mass migration of Danes into England as there had been in the ninth century.
- He issued strict laws which were practical, understandable and helped to keep the peace. They also recognised the distinctiveness of Danish customs in the Danelaw.
- In 1017, he married Emma, Ethelred's widow. She was the sister of the Duke of Normandy, a useful guarantee of peace from that side of the Channel.

▲ An eleventh-century runestone in Sweden. The runes say: 'Alli had this stone raised in memory of himself. He took Cnut's payment in England. May God help his spirit'

> ## Reflect
>
> Which of the measures above do you think would most help to bring peace to England?

Cnut and the Church

Cnut put considerable effort and money into building good relations with the English Church. He treated pagans with tolerance in Scandinavia, but in England he worked hard to develop the Church.

He gave land and important relics to monasteries. The relics brought pilgrims and their journeys encouraged trade. He exempted the town of Canterbury from geld payments as a way of apologising for the murder of Archbishop Aelphege by Vikings in 1012. He even did penance for the murder of King Edmund in 869 (see page 57) by setting up a monastery at Bury St Edmunds.

Winchester was Cnut's capital city. This image from a bible at Winchester records how King Cnut and Queen Emma presented a fine gold cross for the altar at a new church there. The drawing shows how God favours them: at the top are Christ with the Virgin Mary and St Peter; below them, angels present Emma with a veil and Cnut with a crown: below them are the grateful monks of Winchester.

Good relations with the Church brought Cnut benefits, of course. Other kings and the Pope, who had been doubtful about the faith of Harald Bluetooth and Svein Forkbeard, accepted him as a true Christian. Above all, the Anglo-Saxon archbishops, bishops and clergy supported him throughout his reign. This, along with his new laws and his armed forces, gave England a period of great stability.

▲ An illustration from the eleventh-century Winchester Bible. The image of Cnut is the earliest picture we have of any named Viking

Cnut: a European king

England was always Cnut's main power-base but between 1018 and his death in 1035, he developed what some historians have called a northern European or Anglo-Scandinavian empire. However, he made little attempt to unite his kingdoms, treating them all separately as family possessions.

As well as taking land, he also increased his influence and reputation among other rulers and regions as this panel shows.

Scotland, the Islands and Ireland
By 1031, Cnut had persuaded the King of Scotland and the ruler of the Isle of Man to accept him as their overlord.

The rulers of Orkney and the other islands were also his vassals.

His lordship in these regions helped to keep the western and northern fringes of England free from violence. As is often the case, peace also helped trade.

Denmark
Cnut's brother Harald, who had seized the throne of Denmark on Svein's death, died in 1018. Cnut crossed the North Sea in person to ensure that he now became king of Denmark. His kingdom there included the area of southern Sweden known as Scania, just east of Denmark. After his coronation, he returned to England.

Scania and the Baltic Sea
In 1021, Thorkell the Tall was back in his homeland in Scania. Once there, he caused more trouble so Cnut sailed back to Denmark and spent two years subduing him. This brought Scania much more closely under Danish control than ever before. Cnut gained control of the trade routes between the North Sea and the Baltic. He also made himself overlord of part of Sweden and formed an alliance with Poland. This benefited English trade with the Baltic, particularly through York (Jorvik).

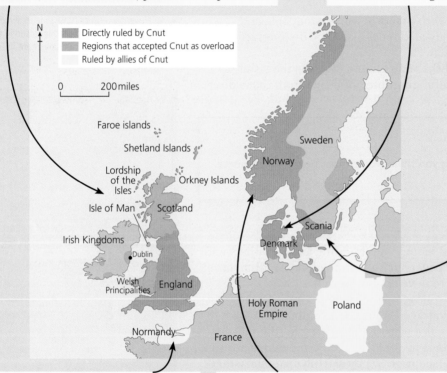

Map key:
- Directly ruled by Cnut
- Regions that accepted Cnut as overload
- Ruled by allies of Cnut

N

0   200 miles

Faroe islands

Shetland Islands

Lordship of the Isles

Isle of Man

Orkney Islands

Scotland

Irish Kingdoms

Dublin

Welsh Principalities

England

Normandy

France

Holy Roman Empire

Norway

Sweden

Scania

Denmark

Poland

Normandy
In 1017, Cnut's marriage to Emma, sister of the Duke of Normandy, helped to keep peace and encourage trade across the English Channel.

Norway
Svein Forkbeard had always claimed some of Norway as part of his realm, but by 1015 a Norwegian warrior called Olaf Haraldson had declared himself king. He was a Christian (of some sort) who tried to convert the nation. His tactics were ruthless: those who refused to convert were blinded or executed and pagan sites were defiled. In 1026, with England secure, Cnut sailed to Scandinavia and began his campaign against Olaf. In 1028 Cnut became king of all Norway, driving Olaf out of the country. When Olaf tried to return with an army in 1030 he was defeated and killed. In later years, Olaf became both a saint and a national hero in Norway for establishing the Christian church there and for giving the country unity and its first twelve years of independence, free of outside influence.

Reflect

What does this chart show about the ways in which Cnut increased his land and influence?

Recognition in Rome

In 1027, even while he was in the middle of his war with Olaf in Norway, Cnut visited Rome. He was attending the coronation of the German Holy Roman Emperor Conrad II. The coronation was a splendid and colourful occasion, with visiting kings, dukes, bishops and archbishops from all over western Christianity. Cnut stood shoulder to shoulder with them and received their recognition as the greatest monarch in Europe other than the Holy Roman Emperor himself. It must have been the high point of his life and he wrote to his people on the way home, describing himself as 'King of all England and Denmark and the Norwegians and of some of the Swedes'.

The end of an era

Cnut died at Shaftesbury in 1035, aged only 40, and was buried at Winchester. He was succeeded by first one and then another of his sons but neither had his skill as a king. By 1042, they had lost first Norway and then England. An Anglo-Saxon, Edward the Confessor, became King of England. The line of 'Great Danes' had ended.

> **Reflect**
>
> Why do you think Cnut made a point of attending Conrad's coronation?

◀ This chest at Winchester Cathedral is believed to hold the bones of King Cnut … along with those of many others. During the English Civil War, soldiers smashed the tombs of Cnut and others buried there. All the scattered bones were collected and placed in this seventeenth-century chest

Record

Finish your final summary sheet by filling in the pie chart as described on page 83.

Review

Look at your three summary sheets and their pie charts.

- For each of the three Danish kings, list three adjectives that you think best describe the qualities he showed as a king.
- Choose the king who you think was the greatest of these 'Great Danes'. Explain why you made that selection, using details from his career to support your opinion. You will need to make it clear what makes a king of that period 'great'.

Remembering the Vikings

▲ Members of the American group, the 'Independent Order of Vikings', in the nineteenth century

The age of Viking expansion gradually came to an end in about 1050. There were raids on England in the 1070s, but they were driven off. No more journeys were made to unknown lands. Kings ruled in Scandinavia as they did across western Europe. Christianity became rooted in people's lives. For many centuries, when the Viking past was remembered, it was seen as barbaric, wild, brutal and pagan.

In the nineteenth century, however, the people of Scandinavia began to look at their past differently, often as a reaction against the rapid modernisation which was just beginning to take place. Young Swedes met to drink mead from drinking horns, call each other by Viking names, recite verses from the *eddas* (see page 20) and to write their own poetry in the same style. Some of the paintings you have seen in this book date from this time, as artists tried to portray key moments from the Viking past (see, for example, pages 60 and 77).

Many Scandinavians emigrated to the USA in the nineteenth century and some kept memories of their homelands alive by forming social clubs, dressing up in what they thought the Vikings wore, like the members of the 'Independent Order of Vikings' shown in the photograph above.

The group still exists today.

Some people are fascinated by Viking achievements and seek to recreate them.

When the Gokstad ship burial was excavated in 1880 and the Oseberg ship in 1904, it created huge public interest in these real and powerful pieces of evidence of their Viking past. A reconstruction of the Gokstad ship was made and sailed to America in 1893. In 1998, just about a thousand years after Leif Eriksson is believed to have reached North America, a group of Americans built a replica of the type of ship they think he used and sailed it from Greenland to L'Anse aux Meadows in Newfoundland.

On a more humble level, a growing number of people enjoy being Viking re-enactors. Many take enormous care to make their clothing, tools and weapons as accurate as possible.

The Shetland Islands were among the first places outside Scandinavia to be settled by Vikings, and Shetlanders are very aware of their heritage. A mid-winter ceremony called 'Up Helly Aa' was started in 1881 and continues to the present. The celebrations take place under the leadership of a jarl and they culminate in the burning of a full-scale replica Viking longboat, as seen here.

▲ A Viking re-enactor at the Jorvik festival, 2015

▼ The Up Helly Aa celebrations in Shetland, 2013

Preparing for the examination

The world period study forms the first half of Paper 3: world history. It is worth 20 per cent of your GCSE. To succeed in the examination, you will need to think clearly about different aspects of Viking Expansion, c. 750–1050 and to support your ideas with accurate knowledge. This section suggests some revision strategies and explains the types of examination questions that you can expect.

Summaries of the five issues

Your study of Viking Expansion, c. 750–1050 has covered five important issues:

1. Homelands
2. Volga Vikings
3. Raiders and invaders
4. Settlers
5. Kings

To prepare for the examination it will help to produce clear and accurate summary notes for each issue.

In the specification for your GCSE course, each of these five issues is divided into three sections. We divided each enquiry in this book into three stages to match these sections and to help you build your knowledge and understanding step by step. Your summary notes for each issue will need to cover each of the three sections. Here are four suggestions for structuring your revision notes. Choose the one that is best for you, or use a variety if you prefer.

1. Mind maps

A mind map on A3 paper is a good way to summarise each of the sections for a particular issue. You could use a different colour for each section. Your first mind map might look something like this.

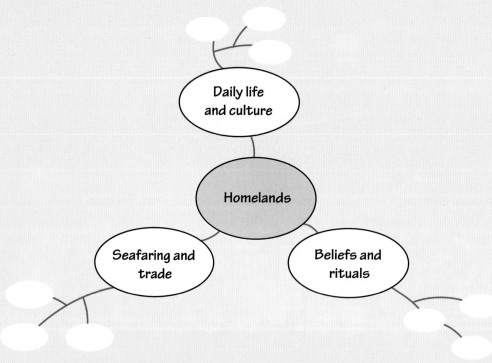

2. Charts

If you find it easier to learn from lists then a summary chart for each issue you have studied might be best for you. You can use the format shown here or design your own. Just make sure that you include clear summary points for each of the three sections in each enquiry you have studied.

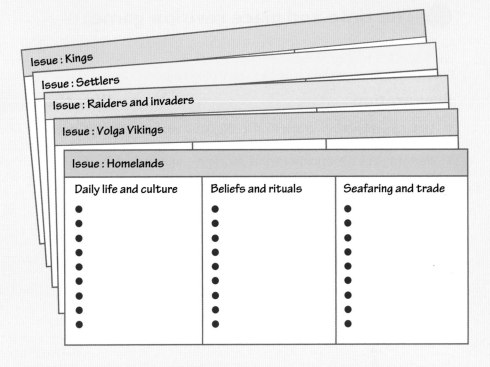

3. Small cards

Small cards are a flexible way to make revision notes. You could create a set of revision cards for each of the five main issues/enquiries you have studied. It would be good to use a different colour for each set of cards.

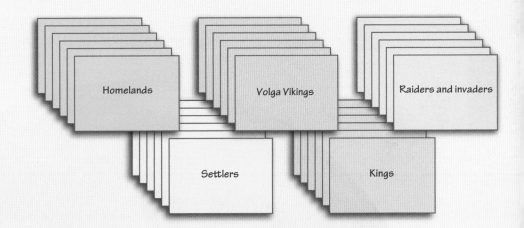

4. Podcasts

If you learn best by listening to information, you could record your knowledge and understanding by producing podcasts to summarise what you have learned about each of the five main issues. You could produce your podcast with a friend using a question-and-answer format.

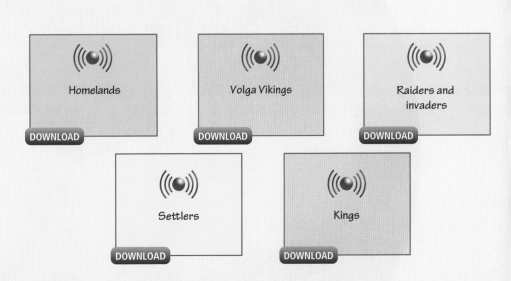

The time and place revision game

In your examination your will need to show a confident knowledge and understanding of what happened; when and where in the story of Viking expansion. This activity should help you. Do the preparation and play the game in groups of four people.

Preparation

1. Make a simple copy of the map and place-name labels shown below.
2. Now prepare five timelines, one for each enquiry. Surround your map with timelines based on those shown here. The one about 'Homelands' has been done for your so you can simply copy it out. The others suggest the first and last entries but you will need to look back at Enquiries 2, 3, 4 and 5 to complete them fully. (The two timelines at the bottom of the page are likely to be the longest.)
3. Stick your map and timelines onto a large sheet of paper.
4. Place the sheet on a table and gather around it.

Play the game

1. With closed eyes, one player must place a finger somewhere on the sheet of paper.
2. If the person's finger lands on the map, he or she must decide which is the nearest named place and then find an event associated with that place on one of the timelines and explain it in more detail. (For example, saying what caused it, what it shows about Viking life or how things were changing, why it was significant or what sort of evidence we have about it.)
3. If the person's finger lands on the timeline, he or she must still explain the event but must also find another event on another timeline that it can be compared or linked to. The player must persuade the others that the link is fair.

Homelands

750	Most Vikings in Scandinavia lived by farming or fishing. As pagans, they believed in many gods
8th century	Population rising in Scandinavia
780s	Kaupang – the first market town in Norway
800	Gokstad ship built
808	Hedeby became the main trading town of Denmark
820	Oseberg ship built

Volga Vikings

c. 780	Vikings trading with Slavs at Staraya Ladoga on river Volkhov
878	King Vladimir of Kiev (a Viking) became a Christian

Raiders and invaders

c. 789	Vikings attack Dorset in southern England
988	King Alfred and King Guthrum make peace and agree that Vikings can live in the Danelaw

Settlers

c. 800	Vikings settle in the Shetland and Orkney Islands
1050	Greenland's Eastern and Western settlements were at their peak

Great Danes (Kings)

958	Harald Bluetooth became King of Denmark
1035	Death of Cnut, King of England, Denmark and Norway

Exam guidance

The world period study forms the first half of Paper 3: world history. It is worth 20 per cent of your GCSE. The whole exam lasts for 1 hour 45 minutes so you will have just over 50 minutes to answer the four questions on Viking Expansion, c. 750–1050.

Question 1

You will be asked three quick questions, each worth one mark. Question 1 requires you to show factual knowledge about Viking Expansion, c. 750–1050. The questions will usually begin 'Give **one** example of ...', 'Name **one** ...', 'Which ...?', 'Name the ...', 'What was ...?'

Example

I. a Name one Viking god. (1)
   b Name one of the major rivers that Vikings used to sail deep into Russia. (1)
   c Name one country that was ruled by King Cnut as part of his empire. (1)

Make a list of ten questions which would make a good Question 1.

Question 2

This question is worth nine marks. It will always begin 'Write a clear and organised summary of ...'. You might be asked to write a narrative account of how an aspect of Viking Expansion, c. 750–1050 changed over time or a particular description of an aspect of Viking Expansion, c. 750–1050 at a particular time.

Example

2. Write a clear and organised summary that analyses Viking contact with the Arab world. Support your summary with examples. (9)

Think of five more good questions for the summary task.

Question 3

This is an explanation task worth ten marks. Typical questions will begin 'Why ...', 'Why did ...?', 'What was the impact of ...?', 'What caused ...?', 'Why do you think ...?'

Example

3. What caused Viking raids in the west between 793 and 850? Explain your answer. (10)

Think of five more good questions for the explanation task.

Question 4/5

The last question in the first part of Paper 1 is the most challenging because it asks you to make a judgement about an aspect of Viking Expansion, c. 750–1050. You need to save enough time for this question because it is worth eighteen marks. You have a choice of two questions. The question will always ask you 'how far' you agree with a given statement.

Examples

4. 'The study of Viking society in their homelands of Scandinavia shows us that they were much more than just warriors.' How far do you agree with this statement? Give reasons for your answer. (18)
5. How far do you agree that the Vikings were quickly converted to Christianity? Give reasons for your answer. (18)

Think of five more good questions for the judgement task.

Glossary

Abbasid family that ruled Baghdad and much of the Muslim world from 750 to 1258

Althing The Icelandic national assembly where important decisions about were made by all free men

amber a hard orange substance made from tree resin that has fossilised. Often used to make jewellery.

archaeologist person who studies the past by finding and studying the remains of objects and buildings

aristocrat a noble such as a duke or earl

Asgard place where the Viking gods lived

bazaar market

berserker a type of ferocious Viking warrior who wore a bear-skin in battle

blot a Viking sacrifice

bondi freeemen i.e. men who farmed their own land

boss (shield-boss) the central part of a Viking shield

burh a fortified Anglo-Saxon town

Byzantine relating to the Byzantine Empire, the Greek-speaking eastern half of the Roman Empire that had its capital city at Constantinople, (modern-day Istanbul in Turkey).

Caliph title of a Muslim ruler

Caliphate area   ruled by a Muslim caliph

chronicle a written record of past events

convert/conversion to change religion

cultivable land suitable for growing crops

culture way of life

Danegeld protection money paid by Saxons to bribe Vikings not to attack their lands

Danelaw large parts of eastern England where Viking law and culture were establsihed after they settled the area in the late ninth century A.D.

deity a god

dirham an Arabic coin

DNA a type of acid (deoxyribonucleic acid) in every living creature that carries information about its genes e.g. its ancestry

draught the depth of a ship in the water

drekke a very large Viking longship

eddas Viking folk stories

ermine the fur of a stoat

estuary the mouth of a river where the water is tidal

eunuch a man, often a servant, who has been castrated

fertile productive, e.g. land where crops grow easily

fjord deep sea inlets along the coast of places such as Norway and Greenland

fossilised an object turned to stone over a long period of time

Frankish something related to the tribes known as Franks

Franks/Frankish members of the German tribes that lived in the lands now known as France and Germany

Frey Viking god of good weather and prosperity

Freya Viking goddess of love and magic

futhark the Viking alphabet

geld a type of tax paid by Anglo-Saxons

heathen person who does not accept a religion that says there is only one God

Hel place where evil creatures such as trolls lived, according to Viking beliefs

hoard a hidden collection of coins or treasure

hogback tombstone a stone burial marker with a rounded top looking like the back of a pig

Holy Roman Emperor the ruler of the Holy Roman Empire

Holy Roman Empire a large area of small states in central Europe that grew out of Charlemagne's Frankish Empire. It was loosely based on the old Roman Empire and had its own emperor.

hörgr an altar where offerings were made to Viking gods

housecarls a warrior who served as a professional bodyguard to a king or noble

jarl a chief who was the most important bondi (freeman) in an area

jetty a structure at which boats can tie up at a river's edge

karvi a small Viking longship

knarr a wide Viking sailing ship used for longer journeys carrying people, livestock and other goods

lathe machine for making round wooden objects such as bowls

Lið a fighting unit in a Viking chief's army

loom a machine for weaving cloth

midden rubbish tip

Midgard place where humans live, according to Viking beliefs

mint place where coins are made

monastery home of a community of monks

napalm a sticky substance that burns fiercely

Norn a Viking-style language spoken by people living in the Shetland and Orkney islands until the eighteenth century

norns three female creatures who controlled the past, present and future according to Viking beliefs

Norse relating to the people of Scandinavia, especially Norway

Odin the Vikings' supreme god

Orthodox Church name given to the Christian Church in eastern Europe and Russia

overlord a ruler to whom others swear loyalty

pagan person who believes in more than one god

pendant piece of jewellery that hanges e.g. from a cord around the neck

Picts tribe that lived in Scotland in the Viking era and earlier

Ragnarok the battle at which the world will end, according to Viking beliefs

re-enactor person who tries to re-create and act out the life-style of people from the past

ritual religious activities usually carried out in a serious and solemn way

rums sets of benches in a Viking ship on which of which a rower sat

runes Viking writing

runestone stone engraved with Viking writing in runes

Rus name given to the Vikings who traded and settled in the east

sable very fine fur from a weasel-like animal living in Siberia in the north of Russia

saga an Icelandic long story about Viking heros, originally spoken but later written down

Scandinavia term used for the lands of modern-day Denmark, Norway and Sweden

seax a large knife

skald a Viking poet

skeid a large Viking warship

skraeling barbarian or outsider

slag waste material produced when making metal objects

Slav a member of the group of people who live in eastern Europe

snekkja a small Viking warship

tactics plans of attack

thing local assemblies where Viking freemen met to make important decisions

Thor Viking god of thunder, lightning and law and order

thrall slave

Varangian a name given by eastern Europeans to Vikings; the Varangian Guard were Viking warriors who acted as bodyguards to the Byzantine Emperor

vassal a person who swore loyalty to an overlord

vestments clothing worn by priests during religious ervices

Viking name given to people from Scandinavia who went 'viking' or raiding by sea

wharf a level platform, built so that ships can tie up at the edge of a river or the sea.

whetstone stone used for sharpening tools and weapons

Yggdrasil a sacred ash tree that was at the centre of the universe according to Viking beliefs

Index

Acknowledgements

p.6 Vikings, Jackson, Peter (1922–2003)/Private Collection/© Look and Learn/Bridgeman Images; **p.7** © ixpert – Shutterstock; **p.8** *t* © Reto Stöckli, NASA Earth Observatory, *b* © Johnny Madsen/Alamy Stock Photo; **p.9** *t* © Andrey Armyagov – Shutterstock, *b* © mkant – Shutterstock; **p.10** *t* Reconstruction of a Viking Farm, Moesgaard, Denmark (photo)/Jean-Pierre Courau/Bridgeman Images, *b* © Andrea Magugliani/Alamy Stock Photo; **p.11** *t* © ALEXANDER V EVSTAFYEV – Shutterstock, *b* Museum of Cultural History, Oslo; **p.12** © Richard T. Nowitz – Getty Images; **p.13** *t* © Heritage Image Partnership Ltd/Alamy Stock Photo, *b* © Lennart Larsen/National Museum of Denmark; **p.14** *t* © Cindy Hopkins/Alamy Stock Photo, *c* © Granger Historical Picture Archive/Alamy Stock Photo, *b* Roberto Fortuna & Kira Ursem/National Museum of Denmark; **p.15** © Berig via Wikipedia Commons (https://en.wikipedia.org/wiki/GNU_Free_Documentation_License); **p.16** *t* © Pascal Volk – Flickr (https://creativecommons.org/licenses/by-sa/2.0/), *b* © World History Archive/Alamy Stock Photo; **p.17** © HENNING BAGGER/AFP/Getty Images; **p.18** *l* & *r* copyright unknown; **p.19** *tr* © Ted Spiegel – Getty Images, *tc* © De Agostini Picture Library – Getty Images, *b* Kaupang Harbour: Flemming Bau; **p.20** Detail of figures illustrating a saga, from the Isle of Gotland (stone), Viking, (9th century)/Historiska Museet, Stockholm, Sweden/Bridgeman Images; **p.21** © Heritage Image Partnership Ltd/Alamy Stock Photo; **p.22** *t* copyright unknown, *b* © Per Poulsen/National Museum of Denmark; **p.23** © imageBROKER/Alamy Stock Photo; **p.24** *t* © Peter Barritt/Alamy Stock Photo, *b* © Yvette Cardozo/Alamy Stock Photo; **p.25** *t, c* & *b* © Museum of Cultural History, University of Oslo; **pp.26–7** © Svetlana Bobrova – Shutterstock; **p.28** © Wilson44691 via Wikipedia Commons ((https://en.wikipedia.org/wiki/GNU_Free_Documentation_License)); **p.30** *tl* © PRISMA ARCHIVO/Alamy Stock Photo, *clt* © DONOT6_STUDIO- Shutterstock, *clb* © Warren Metcalf – Shutterstock, *bl* © York Archaeological Trust, *tr* © Amelie Koch – Shutterstock, *cr* © Arterra/UIG via Getty Images, *br* © Christer Åhlin, The Swedish History Museum; **p.31** *t* copyright unknown, *b* © Håkan Henriksson via Wikipedia Commons (https://creativecommons.org/licenses/by/3.0/); **p.33** © Tåggas via Wikipedia Commons (https://creativecommons.org/licenses/by-sa/3.0/deed.en); **p.34** *tl* & *r* © University of Oslo, *bl* © The Swedish History Museum; **pp.36–7** copyright unknown; **pp.38** & **39** public domain; **p.41** © W.carter via Wikipedia (https://creativecommons.org/licenses/by-sa/4.0/); **p.42** *t* © Richard Dunwoody/Alamy Stock Photo, *b* Cott Nero D IV f.27 Incipit page to the Gospel of St. Matthew with decorated letters 'LIB', from the Lindisfarne Gospels, 710-721 (vellum), English School, (8th century)/British Library, London, UK/© British Library Board. All Rights Reserved/Bridgeman Images; **p.43** © Danita Delimont/Getty Images; **p.45** © Juan Marcos Canela/Alamy Stock Photo; **p.46** public domain; **p.47** © Johnbod / https://commons.wikimedia.org/wiki/File:St_Ninian's_Isle_TreasureDSCF6214.jpg/https://creativecommons.org/licenses/by-sa/3.0/deed.en; **p.48** *t* © Agencja Fotograficzna Caro/Alamy Stock Photo, *b* © Wolfgang Sauber via Wikipedia Commons (https://creativecommons.org/licenses/by-sa/4.0/deed.en); **p.49** © Chris Hellier/Alamy Stock Photo; **p.50** *t* © The Sea Warriors (gouache on paper), English School, (20th century)/Private Collection/© Look and Learn/Bridgeman Images, *b* © CM Dixon/Print Collector/Getty Images; **p.51** *t* © Dominic Zschokke via Wikipedia (https://creativecommons.org/licenses/by-sa/4.0/deed.de), *c* © Hilt of a Viking sword found at Hedeby, Denmark, 9th century (iron)/Schleswig-Holsteinischen Museum, Kiel, Germany/Bridgeman Images, *b* © Museum of London; **p.52** *t* © Mim Friday/Alamy Stock Photo, *bl* © PRISMA ARCHIVO/Alamy Stock Photo, *br* © World History Archive/Alamy Stock Photo; **p.53** © Oxford Archaeology; **p.54** © Loop Images Ltd/Alamy Stock Photo; **p.55** © World History Archive/Alamy Stock Photo; **p.58** © Viking Archaeology (http://viking.archeurope.info); **p.60** VIKINGS PLUNDERING a monastery. Panel, 1883, by Lorenz Frolich/Granger Historical Picture Archive; **p.61** *t* © National Geographic Stock: Vintage Collection/Granger, NYC — All rights reserved., *b* © Everett Collection Inc/Alamy Stock Photo; **p.62** © ARCTIC IMAGES/Alamy Stock Photo; **p.64** © CM Dixon/Print Collector/Getty Images; **p.65** © Jonathan Mitchell/TopFoto; **p.67** *t* © Geograph, *bl* © David Coleman/Alamy Stock Photo, *br* © British Museum; **p.68** *t* © www.dublincastle.ie, *b* © INTERFOTO/Alamy Stock Photo; **p.69** © Carolyn Clarke/Alamy Stock Photo; **p.70** © Paul White – Real Yorkshire/Alamy Stock Photo; **p.71** *t* & *b* © York Archaeological Trust; **p.72** *all* © York Archaeological Trust; **p.73** © British Museum; **p.74** © andrej polivanov/Alamy Stock Photo; **p.75** © John Tlumacki/The Boston Globe via Getty Images; **p.76** © Prisma by Dukas Presseagentur GmbH/Alamy Stock Photo; **p.77** *t* Althing in Session (oil on canvas), Collingwood, William Gersham (1854-1932)/Private Collection/Bridgeman Images, *b* © Michele Burgess/Alamy Stock Photo; **p.78** *t* © Werner Forman/Universal Images Group/Getty Images, *b* © Paul Nicklen – Getty Images; **p.79** © Robert Bird/Alamy Stock Photo; **p.80** © Árni Magnússon Institute; **p.81** © Heritage Image Partnership Ltd/Alamy Stock Photo; **pp.82** & **83** © Tobias Bondesson/Museum Vestsjælland; **p.84** Via http://viking.archeurope.info/i; **p.85** *t* © De Agostini/G. Wright. - Getty Images, *b* © Granger Historical Picture Archive/Alamy Stock Photo; **p.86** © Alex_Murphy – Shutterstock; **p.87** © Yann Arthus-Bertrand – Getty Images; **p.88** © Nationalmuseets Samlinger (https://creativecommons.org/licenses/by-sa/2.5/dk/); **p.89** © Chronicle/Alamy Stock Photo; **p.90** © Oxford Archaeology; **p.92** © Sonia Halliday Photo Library/Alamy Stock Photo; **p.93** Danes arrive in England/British Library, London, UK/© British Library Board. All Rights Reserved/Bridgeman Images; **p.94** © CM Dixon/Print Collector/Getty Images; **p.95** *t* © Berig via Wikipedia Commons (https://creativecommons.org/licenses/by-sa/3.0/deed.en), *b* © British Library Board. All Rights Reserved / Bridgeman Images; **p.97** © Amanda Slater – Flickr (https://creativecommons.org/licenses/by-sa/2.0/); **p.98** © http://www.hroarr.com/; **p.99** *t* © OLI SCARFF/AFP/Getty Images, *b* © Ken Scicluna – Getty Images; **p.102** © ixpert – Shutterstock.